FATE!
LUCK!
CHANCE!

AMY TAN, STEWART WALLACE,

AND THE MAKING OF

The Bonesetter's Daughter OPERA

FATE!
LUCK!
CHANCE!

BY KEN SMITH

FOREWORD BY ORVILLE SCHELL

CHRONICLE BOOKS

SAN FRANCISCO

For Bee, my own "precious auntie," whose lifelong love of music, literature, and travel is there on every page.

Library of Congress Cataloging-in-Publication Data:
Smith, Ken, 1965–
    Fate! Luck! Chance! : Amy Tan, Stewart Wallace, and the making of The Bonesetter's Daughter opera / by Ken Smith.
    p. cm.
    ISBN 978-0-8118-6605-7
    1. Wallace, Stewart. Bonesetter's Daughter. 2. Tan, Amy. I. Wallace, Stewart. Bonesetter's Daughter. Libretto. II. Title. III. Title: Amy Tan, Stewart Wallace, and the making of The Bonesetter's Daughter opera. IV. Title: Bonesetter's Daughter opera.

ML410.W279S65 2008
782.1—dc22

                              2008014870

Manufactured in the United States of America

Design by Brad Mead.

10 9 8 7 6 5 4 3 2 1

Chronicle Books LLC
680 Second Street
San Francisco, California 94107

www.chroniclebooks.com

CONTENTS

FOREWORD

Operas are usually the work of a composer and a librettist who come from a common cultural tradition. *The Bonesetter's Daughter*, adapted from Amy Tan's 2001 novel, was a very different proposition. Creating the opera tested the collaborative abilities of a group of people who were a veritable U.N. of ethnic and cultural heritages. It could easily have been culture clash. Instead, it resulted in a fascinating project that gained hybrid vigor from its diverse cultural gene pool.

Consider the mix: Amy Tan is a Chinese American from San Francisco. Composer Stewart Wallace is a Jewish American of Russian descent born in Philadelphia and raised in Texas. Director Chen Shi-Zheng, from inland China, is Chinese Chinese gone global. Sarina Tang, the opera's catalyst, is a Franco-Italian Chinese American raised in Brazil. David Gockley, the San Francisco Opera's general director, is a straight-up American with roots in Pennsylvania and Texas. Zheng Cao, the mezzo-soprano playing Ruth and Young LuLing, is a multilingual Chinese from Shanghai. Li Zhonghua, a classical Chinese percussionist, and Qian Yi, the opera's lead female performer and *kunju* singer, are Chinese of the most traditional kind. Even for a self-confessed multicultural opera, that's quite a melting pot to melt!

This cultural hodgepodge bespeaks of exactly the thematic territory that Tan's novels have long sought to explore. And so Tan was much smarter to treat her coterie of collaborators as an open-pit mine of talent from which she, and the opera, could extract a rich vein of artistic ore, rather than as acolytes assigned to provide music and stage sets to foliate her novel's existing text.

Still, some have been confused by the mulatto nature of this opera. As Shi-Zheng understands, "The question will come up at some point: Is this a Chinese opera or a Western opera?"

He quickly answers his own question: "This project exists right at the juncture where we meet," he tells us. "[It] creates a world where both can exist on equal terms."

By merging the once discrete universes of China and America, *The Bonesetter's Daughter* becomes a Sino-American opera, written, composed, directed, and produced by a team that embodies and lives its thematic subject matter. In our rapidly homogenizing world, this kind of interesting new synthesis—where neither side of any divide is allowed to remain in preponderance—is what best exemplifies the new hybrid cultural vigor that can only arise out of a highly spontaneous and interactive process. This process may not have been what the opera's progenitors intended as they set forth on this project, but it is the one that they fortuitously allowed themselves to set off on after they began.

Like the characters in *The Bonesetter's Daughter*, the creators of this opera are fascinated by memory, the same theme that so animates Tan's fiction. It is through the process of regaining memory that the opera's characters, like its creators, find a chance to fuse together their familiar pasts in China to their presents in America.

"What is our connection to our pasts and to our parents and ancestors?" Tan always seems to be wondering. This is also a major focus in traditional Chinese Confucian culture, which stresses the need for the living to remember the departed—indeed, to venerate deceased family members through the rituals of ancestor worship. This emphasis on remaining connected with those who preceded you in any *jia*, or family, through the maintenance of ancestral tablets and temples, family genealogies, and filial devotion was mirrored by the parallel emphasis that traditional Chinese placed on the writing of both "official" and "wild" (unofficial) histories. The fixation on maintaining historical records of almost everything, from the family to the state—in order to better be able to refer readily to the past so as not to repeat its mistakes—meant that memory and remembering were considered among the most fundamental virtues in the grand scheme of classical Chinese culture.

Alas, when China skidded into the twentieth century, so much happened that left people wanting to forget, and so many political forces conspired against remembering, that China's veneration of historical memory and its ability to keep the powers of memory intact fell into a battered state. After all, when times are bad, memory can raise too many painful, unanswerable, and even dangerous questions. Especially in a country like China that has been wracked by poverty, pestilence, war, revolution, and fratricidal conflict, it is not difficult to understand how most people found the process of remembering nothing but added agony. The reason why Amy Tan keeps returning to the need for memory is perhaps because she has the freedom to exercise that fundamentally positive, but in any case deep-seated, psychological sense that healthy human beings cannot escape coming to terms with their pasts, ancestors, cultures, and finally even with history itself.

"What has haunted me about Amy's story is that it's about the past," says Chen Shi-Zheng. "Those of us who lived through the Cultural

Revolution have tried to forget our past. The past is always there, so big that you can't compress it. But Amy's approach to memory is to go back and dig it out, like archaeology. She goes back and opens the wounds because they will always haunt you until you come to terms with them. It starts out as Amy's story, but it becomes the story of everyone who's ever had to carry their past with them."

The Bonesetter's Daughter is not only about the need of human beings to remember. For those who have made precipitous transmigrations of their figurative souls from one universe, country, culture, class, or place to another, it is about the need to somehow reconnect both sides of the divides that have left their lives unresolved.

While American Chinese like Amy Tan are trying to remember and reconnect with the China of their parents, Chinese Chinese like Chen Shi-Zheng are trying to remember and make sense out of their pasts, often very bitter ones, in China itself, at the same time they are attempting to connect these complex pasts to their new American, global futures.

What gives *The Bonesetter's Daughter* such resonance is that as the whirlpool of our newly globalized world swirls ever faster around us, more and more people find themselves in a vortex of unimaginable extreme change where the only means of stabilizing oneself, or of making sense of the plethora of contradictory experiences with which modern lives are driven, is through the tonic of memory.

—Orville Schell

OVERTURE
AND SYNOPSIS

As with many other facets of life, the conception didn't become apparent until sometime after the fact. Everyone connected with *The Bonesetter's Daughter* opera has a slightly different perception of when Amy Tan's 2001 novel first took musical life. In opera, though, the composer's recollections weigh heaviest, and Stewart Wallace traces the germ of their collaboration—not merely his association with the project, but the musical soul of the entire piece—to the birth of the original novel.

Having been invited to write a short piece for Amy's publication party by Sarina Tang, the New York–based art dealer and patron who has been both matchmaker and midwife for the opera, Stewart had intuitively composed an a cappella setting of the first lines of the book without, he maintains, any further knowledge of the story. His approach was more than a tad prophetic, since composer and librettist would later jettison most of the novel's narrative trappings to find its core truth in operatic terms.

That distillation process required far more than just a blue pencil. Over time, the veteran opera composer and first-time librettist developed an organic working style. A story about finding oneself by connecting with China took shape, appropriately enough, by connecting with China, with not just Chinese singers and instrumentalists but also acrobats and designers becoming an integral part of the creative vision. Long before its premiere, the opera had already logged hundreds of thousands of air miles.

Sometime after our second trip to China, Stewart began calling me his "spirit guide," which seemed strangely appropriate. In my fifteen years as a music critic, I'd generally carried out my professional role from the sidelines, which one colleague has described as "coming onto the field after the battle is over and shooting the wounded." For this particular opera, though, I'd served on the frontlines. A more thorough description of services offered would include recommending Hong Kong films, ordering regional delicacies, teaching Chinese drinking etiquette, providing coffee, and giving immediate feedback on trans-Pacific phone calls from a composer singing sketches of a new aria. But until I figure out how to fit all of that on a business card, "spirit guide" will have to do.

The experience put me in the best possible position to observe two supremely collaborative artists and discuss their working process with them at length. Much like Amy's novels, my own account starts somewhere in the middle and requires a couple flashbacks. I first found out about the project in 2004 over a late-afternoon lunch at Balthazar, a trendy SoHo bistro close enough to Stewart's home for him to treat it as an extra living room. Though we'd briefly met in Houston at the 1995 premiere of *Harvey Milk*, his fifth opera and most widely known piece, Stewart and I had really gotten to know each other two years later during the final week of rehearsals for *Hopper's Wife*, which I'd attended on assignment for the *Los Angeles Times*. As tightly focused as *Harvey Milk* was sprawling, *Hopper* began with an unapologetically wacky premise—that the painter Edward Hopper was married to the Hollywood gossip columnist Hedda Hopper. From there, it unfolded into provocative juxtapositions of East and West Coast, rarified and vernacular art, essentially offering a ninety-minute rumination on what it means to be American.

Since that time, Stewart had focused his musical attention on concert works, writing a series of pieces for percussionist Evelyn Glennie, a postmodern concerto grosso for the American Composers Orchestra and the British new-music ensemble Icebreaker, and an electric guitar concerto titled *Skvera* for the National Symphony Orchestra and guitarist Marc Ribot. It was *Skvera* that prompted our fateful meeting at Balthazar, this time for an article for the *Washington Post*. Soon the conversation took another turn entirely.

"Did you hear I'm working on an opera with Amy Tan?" he asked. Somehow my profile of Stewart got written, and somehow Stewart's guitar concerto saw its premiere at Kennedy Center, but from that moment on it became mostly an afterthought.

***

When Stewart finally got around to reading *The Bonesetter's Daughter*, he instantly saw in Amy an even more kindred spirit. They were, in a manner of speaking, making similar journeys from different maps. After a nine-month campaign to persuade Amy to bring *Bonesetter* to the opera stage, Stewart was convinced that as far as personal themes and dramatic structure were concerned, they were already on the same page. There was one major problem: he had no idea what the opera should sound like.

Years before, Stewart had traveled in Israel with Michael Korie for several weeks in preparation for writing *Kabbalah*, a nonnarrative opera about Jewish mysticism that premiered at the Brooklyn Academy of Music's Next Wave Festival in 1989. Years later, his travels to the Ukraine when his wife, Dianne Festa, was the Moscow bureau chief for NBC News had yielded much of the raw material for *Skvera*. This time, he knew that once he got to China, he would find his opera.

Stewart's situation was easy to diagnose, particularly since I'd spent the past several years with a similar affliction. Having followed a generation of Chinese-born composers expanding the palette of Western composed music with elements of Chinese opera and Taoist ritual, I'd spent nearly ten years tracing those elements to their source.

Along the way, I met Joanna Lee, a pianist, musicologist, and general force of nature, who had just embarked on a two-year teaching stint at the University of Hong Kong. After leaving that post, Joanna established herself as a nexus for Western performing artists looking to go to China and for Chinese artists looking to perform in the West. Together we'd embarked on a number of projects, including offering musical advice to film directors and shepherding a recording project of Chinese minority music.

So when Stewart told me over lunch that he and Amy would be going to China with their respective spouses as part of Sarina Tang's birthday celebrations, I realized we had little time to lose. I told him, "You have to meet Joanna."

***

During the course of our subsequent chats, Stewart had become firmly convinced that his best entry into Chinese musical culture was through percussion. That made it simple. With his limited free time, there was only one person he needed to meet: Li Zhonghua, the principal percussionist for the China National Peking Opera Company. Zhonghua had been my own primary contact for all things percussive after a cursory introduction from Guo Wenjing, arguably the most forward-thinking composer living in China. After spending several hours rummaging through the back room of an instrument warehouse to find me a set of cymbals, Zhonghua spent even more time carefully explaining why he'd chosen each piece. Later, I'd come to know him as a superb performer in whose hands even Chinese modernist works sounded like an extension of tradition.

There was one catch: Stewart needed a translator with specialized terminology and linguistic nuance, and Joanna was not available to help. With a bit of notice we were able to assemble a team to fit the bill: the young China hand Alex Beels, a gifted linguist whom Joanna had known from graduate school at Columbia, and the even younger China hand Eli Marshall, then a twenty-six-year-old composer living in Beijing on a Fulbright grant.

By any measure, the sessions were a success. What had started out as a primer on percussion-playing technique took on an entirely new dimension as questions got more specific and Zhonghua's answers began to reveal concepts of Peking Opera structure and narrative vocabulary in clear, digestible morsels. Stewart and Amy had already begun thinking of ways to integrate not just the sonorities but also the form and aesthetics of Chinese opera. Even before they left China, Stewart had asked Zhonghua to be part of the team.

Within weeks of his first sprinkling of Chinese opera, Stewart flew to the Spoleto Festival in Charleston for a full immersion in director Chen Shi-Zheng's nineteen-hour production of *Peony Pavilion*—an uncut historical reconstruction of the Ming Dynasty *kunju* classic that, despite having been banned in Shanghai for reasons never fully explained, went on to have an epoch-making run at Lincoln Center and on the international festival circuit. Stewart quickly became convinced that he'd found his director and also, in the production's lead female performer Qian Yi, his actual bonesetter's daughter.

Soon the sounds of Stewart and Amy's initial trip started appearing on the page. During one of Stewart's periodic listening sessions singing his music to a MIDI simulation of the instrumental score, Joanna again broached the subject of China: "What do you want to see when you go back?" Initially caught by surprise, Stewart quickly rose to the challenge. Following the novel's geographical scope would require tracing LuLing's life from small villages outside Beijing onward to Hong Kong and eventually to San Francisco. Beyond that, Stewart had two major goals: to work in greater detail with Zhonghua and to learn as much about as many kinds of Chinese opera as his schedule would allow.

We could work with that, but we had one minor provision: if Stewart really intended to follow his current model, recruiting like-minded people he met along his path, we had many more friends for him to meet.

***

In August 2005 we were about a month away from our two-week musical road trip through China when Joanna, now officially Stewart's "organizer, translator, and bodyguard," got the call. "I need to see funerals," Stewart asked with barely a preamble. Amy might be able to evoke Chinese rituals for a reading audience, but re-creating weddings and funerals on stage was another matter entirely. Clearly the recordings and a copy of *Plucking the Winds*, a newly published musicological study on village life in Shanxi, hadn't been enough.

"You want me to kill somebody?" Joanna asked, incredulously.

"Whatever it takes."

Our group of thirteen, including Amy and her husband, Lou DeMattei, Sarina Tang, and a handful of early supporters of the *Bonesetter* opera project, were scheduled to depart from Beijing on September 17, with Stewart arriving a week earlier to see Chinese opera and work with Zhonghua. Our biggest problem with Stewart, the quintessential type-A New Yorker, had been keeping him from filling every waking moment ahead of time. In China, where you constantly need to accommodate the unexpected, it is better to allow enough room in the schedule for improvisation and serendipitous discoveries like Zhonghua.

Our funeral situation was just such an example. An e-mail to *Plucking the Winds* author Stephen Jones had yielded the name of his research assistant in China. A series of phone calls and a brief face-to-face meeting in Beijing finally produced the desired results. "It's your lucky day—two funerals," Joanna told our now-hesitant composer a few hours before he was due to leave for China.

Although Stewart had gleaned quite a bit from his previous trip— including the need to get out of the cities to see anything of relevance to Amy's story—it was clear that he was heading into an entirely new level of cultural interaction. This time, he was primed both to see traditional Chinese music and to gauge the quality of China's Western-trained musicians. Whether we were at a Peking Opera performance at Beijing's Poly Theatre or a violin recital at the Central Conservatory, the day would extend well into the evening with wide-ranging conversations with artists over dinner and copious red wine.

Stewart and Amy had already established serendipity as a crucial part of their process, and Joanna and I did what we could to help it along. Our list of friends for Stewart had to fulfill two qualifications: a solid grounding in their tradition, either Chinese or Western, and a desire to interact culturally with others. At the top of the list was Wu Tong, the wind instrument virtuoso in Yo-Yo Ma's Silk Road Ensemble, who was more famous at home in Beijing as the founding vocalist for one of China's most popular metal bands.

Mezzo-soprano Ning Liang was a different case entirely. With mothers always being the most memorably idiosyncratic characters in Amy's fiction, the role of LuLing would require a strong presence. That said, Stewart was still taken aback at their initial meeting when Ning burst out, "I don't play old women," leaving the normally hyperverbal composer at a loss for words. Stewart quickly mobilized his charm offensive and, within days, asked Ning to prepare the opera's Prologue with two of her students for a fund-raising event at the end of our trip in Hong Kong. After an impromptu working session in Ning's Beijing apartment, and later recording the *Bonesetter* Prologue in New York, she officially became part of the *Bonesetter* family.

***

"Plucking the winds" is how the Chinese describe fieldwork, and three days after arriving in Beijing, Stewart started plucking a few winds of his own. Later our entire group would travel through western China, from the highly commercialized "ancient town" of Fenghuang in Hunan (a recommendation of Hunan native Chen Shi-Zheng) to the remote eco-museum of Dimen in Guizhou (a six-hundred-year-old minority village converted into a living research center by Lee Wai Kit, a Hong Kong businessman and publisher turned Chinese museum director). But it was the village funerals in Shanxi that would make the strongest impression.

Our destination was Yangjiabu, a small village nearly two hours outside the county town of Datong, the closest marker on the map. Having arrived sometime around 4 P.M.—our "four-hour" drive from Beijing having lasted more than seven, thanks to the burgeoning traffic congestion—we were greeted at the edge of the paved road by Fifth Brother of the Hua family, who escorted us for about 150 yards of ear-splitting fireworks until we reached the first signs of ceremony. Outside a communal courtyard, neighbors had gathered around the Hua Family Shawm Band, a group of semiprofessional musicians who would perform later that year in Amsterdam at the Concertgebouw's China Festival. Village ceremonies like this, however, were their regular gig.

Stewart was immediately taken with the performance, a fiery ensemble of percussion and *suona*, the Chinese reed trumpet. Soon I would understand why—he'd already composed a ceremonial dance featuring precisely this instrumentation—but for the moment we were ensnared by boisterous playing immediately reminiscent of modern jazz and Bulgarian wedding bands, yet very much of a piece with our surroundings.

A tall black-clad Westerner hardly goes unnoticed in a Chinese village, and Stewart often walked a fine line between observing the festivities and becoming part of the show himself. As we followed the procession into the courtyard, where the Taoist priests were carrying on the ceremony proper, Stewart at one point became so touched by the occasion that he sang a funeral tribute in Hebrew, much to the befuddlement of the deceased's husband.

Our road trip through Hunan and Guizhou would later yield additional riches. Now well attuned to spotting funerals, we stumbled upon several more and were always invited in. One night in Zhenyuan, Guizhou, Stewart and I were called over to drink and smoke with friends of the family at the start of a three-night vigil, just after a young relative had burst into a drunken solo recitation from *The Three Kingdoms*.

Minority villages proved less valuable musically, although Stewart would later incorporate the low drones of the *lusheng*, a Miao mouth organ, in his *Bonesetter* orchestration, and was so fascinated with the polyphonic singing of the Dong people that he would later adapt their vocal techniques in his choral writing.

It was the general way of life in the minority villages that offered the greatest illumination. In remote Guizhou, peasant traditions that have long died out in the cities—and even in villages within television range—still carry on, however precariously. Dimen village, which has traditions like papermaking and textile dyeing still in place, as well as scholars and staff to help explain them, won a warm place in our group's collective heart. It was particularly gratifying that when Joanna and I announced our wedding retreat in Dimen the next year, several members of our original group—including Amy, who had been onsite researching an article about the village for *National Geographic* magazine—again braved two flights and a ten-hour bus ride to join us.

"I can't believe that you're going on your honeymoon with my husband," Stewart's wife, Dianne, exclaimed when she heard that Joanna and I were planning an additional few days of fieldwork after Dimen to hear Sichuan opera in Chengdu and *kunju* in Suzhou, its historic birthplace. "I'm not sure *I'd* even do that again," she added, laughing.

But we did. *The Bonesetter's Daughter* was that kind of project.

***

The conversations in this book did not exist in nature. Rather like a musical recording, they were compiled from multiple takes, spliced and edited to give the flavor of a genuine dialogue in real time. Several comments were taken from public forums, including a public event at the Asia Society in New York. Most were made either in private or among a select, informal audience. Sometimes multiple speakers were in the same room, goading each other on. Most often, the semblance of personal interaction was facilitated by e-mail and the occasional conference call.

SYNOPSIS OF THE OPERA

Because the story as it transpires in the opera has been reduced, compressed, and in some cases highly altered from the original novel, we offer a synopsis of the opera.

PROLOGUE—DRAGON DANCE

(A TIMELESS VOID)

Out of the fog, three women emerge: Ruth, a modern, American-born Chinese woman; LuLing, Ruth's mother, an immigrant woman from a previous generation; and Precious Auntie, a disfigured ghost from another world, clutching a dragon bone.

ACT 1, SCENE 1

(FOUNTAIN COURT RESTAURANT, SAN FRANCISCO, 1997)

A family has gathered for Chinese New Year: Ruth; her mother, LuLing; her husband, Art; her stepdaughters; her in-laws; and an unseen ghost with a disfigured face. Ruth has chosen dishes symbolizing a lucky and harmonious family, but her husband's family rejects each dish. LuLing despairs at her daughter's timidity. Sensing her mother's agitation, Ruth unveils her birthday gift—a mink coat, which her relatives immediately condemn. But LuLing is overjoyed by the gift. When Ruth's in-laws are impressed with how clearly LuLing expresses her thanks, Art proudly announces that Ruth is ghostwriting a book with a lawyer from the O.J. Simpson trial. LuLing offers to help, claiming she was with O.J. at the murder scene. As she re-enacts what she saw, everyone realizes LuLing is losing her mind. Angered that no one believes her, LuLing threatens to kill herself. Storming away, she falls and is mortally injured. Ruth, now feeling guilty, cradles LuLing until the ambulance arrives. Art assures Ruth she is not to blame since her mother has threatened suicide since Ruth's childhood. He offers to get the car, leaving Ruth utterly alone. Suddenly, the ghost, her face now unblemished, caresses Ruth's cheek. She cloaks Ruth in the garb of another era, and Ruth becomes her mother as a young woman. They follow a retinue of dead bodies leaping to the chants of a Taoist monk: "The dead must return home." And so, they return to the village of Immortal Heart, where they will relive the tragedy that binds them.

ACT 1, SCENE 2

(IMMORTAL HEART, A VILLAGE OUTSIDE BEIJING, 1930S)

Chang, the coffin maker, extorts money from mourners, claiming that ancestor ghosts will haunt the cheapskates. Later at the Wang household's ink-making studio, Chang leers at a slave girl, Young LuLing, who is delighted by the attention. Another maid, known as Faceless One, spits at Chang and drags Young LuLing away. She is the woman Young LuLing calls Precious Auntie, who claims she saved LuLing as a baby from an icy gutter. Chang secretly boasts that he's had his way with this faceless woman, the daughter of the late bonesetter. Now he desires not only Young LuLing but also Precious Auntie's inheritance from her father—a dragon bone promising immortality if ground into medicine, which Chang failed to obtain after murdering the bonesetter. He strikes a bargain with Madame Wang to secure the slave girl as his concubine. Precious Auntie sees the secret barter and warns Young LuLing, but Young LuLing dreams only of a new life as the respected wife of an important man, citing village gossip that Precious Auntie once seduced Chang. Precious Auntie then offers the coveted dragon bone, which Young LuLing gladly accepts as part of her dowry, exactly what her future husband wants. Senseless with despair, Precious Auntie grabs back the dragon bone and puts it to Young LuLing's throat. When Young LuLing screams for her life, Precious Auntie drops the bone, horrified, and runs out of the room. Soon the wedding guests arrive, and as the rituals begin, Precious Auntie suddenly appears, cursing Chang for generations to come and warning that her ghost will carry out the litany of horrors. As she kills herself, flames rise and the whole world is destroyed.

ACT 11, SCENE 1

Young LuLing, now destitute, joins a crowd of people who lost their fate in the war. To earn her living, LuLing sets up shop on the harbor, writing letters for abandoned wives. As a storm scatters the crowd, LuLing seeks shelter among the crates. She hears a man's sweet voice calling to her, asking her to write a love letter. Precious Auntie screams unheard, trapped in a void, while Old LuLing in the present world rises from her hospital bed and watches her past unfold. Young LuLing soon recognizes the voice as Chang's and the crates around her as his coffins. He throws her atop a coffin, and as she defends herself with the dragon bone, Chang now has all he desires. As he is about to commence the rape, Precious Auntie furiously breaks free of her confines, throwing Chang to the ground. With the sharp dragon bone, she slices his face, chest, and crotch while extracting a confession about how Chang murdered her father, raped her, and was about to rape his own daughter. Young LuLing now realizes that Precious Auntie and Chang are her parents. As Precious Auntie comforts Young LuLing, Old LuLing joins them in a trio of mutual understanding.

ACT 11, SCENE 2

(HOSPITAL ROOM, SAN FRANCISCO, 1997)

Young LuLing enters the present and becomes Ruth again. She goes to her mother, who is disoriented and approaching death. But in a moment of lucidity she begs Ruth's forgiveness. Precious Auntie, now a luminous vision, approaches LuLing, who calls to her long-lost mother, asking her forgiveness. She motions for the mink coat, and as Ruth puts the coat on Precious Auntie, Precious Auntie places the dragon bone in Ruth's hand, the pain of the past becoming the strength of Ruth's future. Ruth watches as her mother and grandmother merge into the fog.

CHAPTER 1

TRUTH:

SEEKING A TRUE STORY

Artists generally have a touchy relationship with the truth. Take Amy Tan, who puts real words and situations from friends and relatives into the mouths and lives of made-up characters. Or Stewart Wallace, who has taken notably real figures like Edward Hopper and Harvey Milk and made them jump through dramatized and even surreal hoops. Clearly these are artists used to dealing with an advanced definition of the term.

From the time Amy and Stewart began their collaboration on *The Bonesetter's Daughter*, the project was a search for truth in the fundamental sense. In practical terms, it meant that Amy had to distill numerous characters and subplots into a concise, opera-friendly libretto. Stewart needed to grasp the musical essence of a narrative spanning three generations and two continents. What the composer soon realized—and Amy had long known— was that writing about China requires being in China, though what that meant in terms of a musical score would only become clear over time.

Though a longtime veteran of China travel, Amy was a relative new-comer to Chinese music. Stewart, a consummate musical traveler, was getting his first proper introduction to China. Like most Westerners, Stewart first discovered China by way of Chinatown, a particularly urban condition where exposure to the trappings of a culture—like dim sum from a childhood friend's home in Houston—is removed from its original context. Much like Amy's own process, Stewart began with a great many things he already knew were true, then labored to discover why.

Given Amy's relative experience, their travel together was precisely the reverse of what one might expect, with Amy largely—and comfortably—letting Stewart take the lead. Composers often refer to music's function in opera as "the second eye"—the part offering depth and perspective to what is visible on the surface. Particularly on their 2005 trip, Amy was Stewart's "second ear"—the element in the background making sure that his initial musical interests and inclinations were grounded in emotional reality.

Explorers of the old school would famously venture to exotic lands bearing swords. This group, a bit more harried and world-weary, came armed with cameras and recording equipment. Amy's mobile phone was the source of much amusement among minority peasant women, who would leave their planting duties for brief stretches to watch short videos of themselves on the handheld screen. It was a fleeting moment of innocence; by the second trip a year later, mobile phones had become commonplace, even in the rice fields.

Stewart's most valuable commodity turned out to be printed on his business card. Well before he landed in Beijing in 2005, Stewart had heeded suggestions to adopt a proper Chinese name—something that, for a Westerner entering China with limited facility in the language, would suggest a certain pedigree and start things off on the right foot. He became Hui Shi-Zhao (distant, gentle scholar). It was a good summary, he thought, for a composer coming from half a world away to learn from another tradition. Whether in a more formal setting, such as the Peking Opera demonstrations by percussionist Li Zhonghua, or relaxed gatherings like the Mid-Autumn Festival gathering of artists and pop musicians at the home of Chinese rock star Wu Tong, Stewart's Chinese name at least gave people something to talk about before they settled down to more serious matters.

In China, much is in a name: an essential truth that a child is expected to grow into; for adults, a banner they want the world to see. So as "Gentle Scholar" Wallace prepared to join "Beautiful Grace" Tan in search of a musical China, there was yet a third factor to consider: a catalyst from the beginning named Sarina Tang, whose Chinese name, Tang Qi-Feng, translates as "Phoenix Embarking," which pretty much set the tone for the entire endeavor.

1.

BIRTH OF THE PROJECT

SARINA TANG:

The whole project began with friendship. I'd first met Amy and Stewart in 1994 when they were both in residence at Yaddo, a retreat for creative artists, and we all became very close friends. Several years later, when I found out that Amy's novel *The Bonesetter's Daughter* would be published on her birthday, I asked her if I could throw a party. Then I asked Stewart to write a piece of music, and he came up with a short a cappella piece for three female voices.

STEWART WALLACE:

I never told you this, Sarina, but I thought that was a pretty nervy thing to ask at the time. I hadn't even had a chance to read the book, so I just instinctively took the first couple lines and set them for three women. I didn't even know that there were three women characters in the book. This was totally accidental. After I read the book, I thought that it might not be an obvious source for an opera, but the narrative was stirring and deeply emotional in a way that goes far beyond the confines of the story itself. It touched me deeply because it spoke to many things that were close to me: the idea of heritage and destiny, the way we carry our history and family and people in our bones whether we know their stories or not, the idea that those stories affect us, whether or not we've heard them. And the way that we can come together to heal our differences is by coming together with those stories, not just to acknowledge them but to speak them out loud. That was the part of the book I found truly operatic. It speaks to music, and the book as a whole has an inner musical quality. Amy, though, was initially not so convinced.

AMY TAN:

I thought it was a pretty harebrained idea. Maybe Stewart was desperate for ideas at the time, but I had other plans for the story. I knew very little about opera. Not quite on the level of the people who've since asked me, "Do you have to write it in Italian first and translate it?" But pretty close. Eventually, though, I thought, let's humor the man. I do love music. I go to the symphony more often than I do the movies. I had fifteen years of classical piano, so I thought my mother would've approved.

STEWART:

I couldn't let it go, and nine months later I came back and said, "Amy, remember that bit of music I wrote for the party? That is the seed of an opera, and those three women are the bones of the opera. And if we can establish that right at the beginning, we can take this story anywhere."

AMY:

> In many ways, you could say that our having met at Yaddo that summer had a strong bearing on the opera we eventually wrote. It was the summer of the O.J. Simpson trial, which also figured prominently in the novel because Ruth is ghostwriting a book with one of O.J.'s lawyers. Also, when I first met Stewart he was practicing his Chinese. The poet Yang Lian had just taught him his first Chinese phrase—"Wo da ji ba," which means "I have a big dick." Stewart just kept saying this over and over and Yang was laughing his head off. I do think that this was the instigation for several metaphors in the opera when we got to the character of Chang, the coffin maker. But at the time, Stewart was there with his one phrase of Chinese, and I seem to recall some women at Yaddo nodding their heads.

STEWART:

> Oh come on, that was before I was married. And it was a particularly active summer.

AMY:

> I was insulted that nobody hit on me that year. I was truly one of the only people . . .

STEWART:

> Amy was very mischievous. Every weekend she would stock the bar and get a lot of tittie magazines, like *Hot and Over 40*.

AMY:

> I'd stock a full bar—wine, beer, vodka, rum, whisky—so that people could have their cocktail hour. I ended up feeling bad because several people there that year turned out to be recovering alcoholics and one fell off the wagon in a serious way. But yes, there were *Women Over 30, Women Over 40,* and *Women Over 50* that I tucked in with the regular magazines, sometimes with notes inside like "Caught ya!" It was all very juvenile and really fun.

STEWART:

What I most remember about Amy that first year at Yaddo was the night she told us about the friend who was murdered on her birthday, and having to go and identify the body. She wrote an extremely moving essay about that incident in *The Opposite of Fate* and how it led in a way to her becoming a writer. But the trauma of that experience marks many of her stories.

AMY:

What I remember most about Yaddo was the bar in town, where everybody would sit in the garden drinking mint juleps. One night Stewart was singing something from *Harvey Milk* and I thought, this was what being in an artist colony is all about: artists sharing with other people what they'd just created that day. I could never read in public something I'd just written; it would be too threatening. But Stewart started right in singing, and I thought, how wonderful and brave.

STEWART:

Somebody must have asked about it or said something. I wouldn't just launch into something I'd just written for no reason.

AMY:

Oh come on, you do that all the time. You called me once from the airport in New Hampshire.

STEWART:

I was just leaving the MacDowell Colony and had just written what I thought was the end of the opera.

AMY:

I just kept imagining all those people around you at the airport.

STEWART:

That was also the year we first met Sarina. Board members are never allowed to come to Yaddo when the artists are there, but somehow she turned up. And from there on, every time Amy came to New York, Sarina would throw some kind of event.

AMY:

Every time we saw her, I remember feeling that somehow we were orphans and she was the trustee. Sarina was always the person who helped make things happen.

11.
"WHAT DOES IT SOUND LIKE WHEN A GHOST ENTERS?"

SARINA:

Almost always an opera is commissioned by an opera company, but this time we decided to initiate something new. When Amy and Stewart asked me to help make it happen, my first response was, "I have no experience in this." They said, "No one else does, either." So I started thinking about the process as a journey. The story starts in the United States and goes to China, so I thought we would do the same thing for the opera, meaning that we had to go to China in the process, gathering a lot of friends along the way. Still in that initial spirit of friendship, I gathered a number of friends to celebrate my birthday in Shanghai. Amy and Lou and Stewart and Dianne came. As we went on to Chengdu and Beijing listening to Chinese opera, everyone got more and more excited about an opera of *The Bonesetter's Daughter*.

AMY:

I've always felt that if I'm going to write about China, I have to go to China, but at this stage I was leaving myself open to a large range of things. I wasn't going with any specific agenda in mind. I was not a big fan of Chinese music, I should admit. I knew a few pieces like *The Butterfly Lovers*, but they're usually a little over the top for me

emotionally. Chinese opera I didn't understand—I mean I literally didn't understand it: the language, the ritual, the movements.
I had no idea which characters were good and who was evil. I
wasn't that much more schooled in Western opera, but at least I
knew the basic conventions.

STEWART:

> To say I knew nothing about Chinese music would be an understate-
> ment. My first conversation with Ken and Joanna about going to
> China was filled with a lot of *nots*. Joanna asked who I wanted to
> meet, and I said, "not singers, not instrumentalists . . . ." But I did
> want to learn about percussion. I'd used a Chinese cymbal—the
> *xiaoluo* it's called, I know now—in a percussion piece called *The
> Cheese and the Worms* for Evelyn Glennie. You have to understand,
> the original idea was not to do something that reached between
> worlds. I wasn't going to write a "Chinese opera." My music has
> always had a central issue: What does it mean to be American?
> Where do we all come from? Does it matter if we're born here?
> Are we American by virtue of choice? And also, by being American,
> are we open to these things from the rest of the world? I think the
> best part of who we are as Americans is the open part, the part
> receptive to—and, frankly, a product of—all the traditions that
> have settled here. But two things about *Bonesetter* were different
> from the start. The first was working with Amy. The second was
> going to China. By the time we set foot in China, everything
> changed.

AMY:

> When we first met the percussionist, Li Zhonghua, he started play-
> ing through the instruments for Stewart. But pretty soon I started
> asking him narrative questions directly related to the book, like
> "What does it sound like when a ghost enters?" Or, "How does
> someone show that they've just tragically lost someone?" And with
> each of these scenarios Zhonghua would do something specific,
> and I realized that all this music that I thought was just empty ritual

was very much alive. It had emotion and drama and tragedy, with music that was not only harmonious with all its elements but could really tell the story. For me at that point, it was not just seeing where the words and music interact, but also what parts of the story could be felt in the music alone. That's what writers are always looking for: the emotional depth of the story, in whatever way it comes out."

Li Zhonghua:

I first fell in love with traditional opera when I was nine. My parents were big fans and I got my love from them. For the next ten years, I was training to be a Peking Opera actor. But when I was about eighteen, I also discovered percussion, which I started to play even when I was still acting. Percussion opened up a completely different world to me. As an actor you are limited by what one person can portray and suggest, but with a full range of percussion you have literally tens of thousands of different atmospheres on hand that you can create.

Stewart:

As soon as Amy started asking questions, I could see Zhonghua's mind working. He wasn't showing us what he could play—he was showing us his imagination. He was more than just an instrumentalist; he had that entire world in his mind. When Amy asked him about ghosts, he said, "But I'm only one person. I can play only one instrument at a time." I told him, "Just play exactly the same part on each of the four instruments and we'll put it together in our heads." I explained that it's better that way for me as a composer, because I can see how it all fits together. But what he showed us is that everything in the music is so interconnected that we couldn't just import the instruments. I tried to explain my thoughts right there: "We're making an opera based on Amy's book. We came here to learn about Chinese percussion, but at this point, I'm interested in you. Would you be interested in joining us?" He said yes. "Have you ever played with a Western orchestra before?" He said no. And that was where we really began. It was purely in the moment—like many of the moments we had working on the opera, when something just happens.

111.

CHINA: SECOND ACT

STEWART:

After that first trip to China, I started doing a lot of pure research—studying the character types in Chinese opera, watching Hong Kong movies and Chinese film. The movies were initially very helpful. This wasn't new to me, by the way. My immersion point into Hong Kong cinema came years ago with *The Eagle Shooting Heroes*, an action film that has everything and the kitchen sink thrown in. I'd been talking with choreographer Christopher d'Amboise about doing a dance piece on Hong Kong martial arts films back in the early 1990s. So you could say my interest in Chinese opera stems from the cinema. Rhythmically it captures the vibrancy on the streets better than anything I've heard. Soon after we got back from China, Sarina had also urged me to see Chen Shi-Zheng's nineteen-hour production of *The Peony Pavilion*, which is basically a hostage situation for the audience, but also a rigorous, intensive course in Chinese opera. At that point, I realized that Sarina had been right about Shi-Zheng being the perfect director for this project. His *Peony Pavilion* is not traditional Chinese opera. It's a contemporary concept that he brought to the tradition. In a way, it completed our circle, because Amy's and my perspective is very American, and Shi-Zheng's—since he was born in China—is not.

AMY:

We also started looking for singers—or, I should say, Stewart did. I didn't listen to any singers in advance because I had no idea what to look for. All I cared about was that they could emote theatrically.

STEWART:

We didn't do any normal auditions, which are the most mind-numbing part of casting and don't always tell you what a singer can do in any case. I was very impressed with Qian Yi, the principal female singer in *The Peony Pavilion*. Right away, I realized the dramatic potential of having a singer from the world of Chinese opera play the grandmother as the ghost, the voice of tradition, the keeper of the family secrets.

AMY:

More than that, being a *kunju* performer, Qian Yi could immediately solve one of our crucial problems. In the novel, the character of Precious Auntie has no mouth, having been disfigured in a fire. She's unable to talk, which is problematic for an opera. At first, we didn't know if it would be a singing role, but being trained in Chinese opera, Qian Yi could do gestures that would represent her inability to speak.

STEWART:

After that first trip to China, I started writing the Prologue, which has the three voices intermingling in music largely based on the piece I wrote for the publication of Amy's book. I incorporated the Peking Opera percussion I'd learned about from Zhonghua and wrote an opening scene for two *suonas,* the Chinese double-reed trumpet. The sound of the *suona* had floored me at a Sichuan opera performance on our trip with Sarina in Chengdu. The Sichuan opera troupe, I realized later, was pretty touristy, but it was certainly more authentic than the horrible Vegas floor show we saw in Xian.

AMY:

Something that my mother told me before I went to China the first time still rings true: "When you go to China, you will suddenly become Chinese. But when you go to China, no one will think you're Chinese." What she meant was that everything she had told me since my childhood would suddenly become real. But it was true; I was so un-Chinese back then that the only phrase I knew was *ni hao ma* [How are you?].

STEWART:

The trick of writing the Prologue was to write music in my own language that felt Chinese without sounding ersatz Chinese, but first I had to figure out what that meant to me. You can hear it in the timbre and texture, but also in terms of the space between the notes that lets the music resonate with a sense of ritual. The goal was to combine those elements in a way that could be played by a Western orchestra. What I found most startling from that first trip, though, was how much traditional Chinese singing sounds like country music. I had to laugh. Most people say it sounds like screeching—and my own reactions were mixed, depending on the style—but the thing that struck me the most was the stylization of both the vocal production and the physical presentation. In the opening Dragon Dance I was trying to re-create the first sensation I had with Chinese opera, seeing the stage as a container that can barely hold the energy vibrating inside.

* * *

STEWART:

I was still processing what I learned from the first trip when Joanna asked, "What do you want to see when you go back?" In terms of its sound world, the Prologue was a mythical place. For all its Chinese elements, it was a throwback to *Harvey Milk*, narrowing this huge landscape of legacy into a trio of very personal voices. But speaking again with Joanna made me realize how I'd gotten only the broadest strokes of China the first time. Hong Kong sounds totally different from the Chinese countryside, each made up of different strains. I thought about it and realized that for my second trip I needed to see the country purely through music.

AMY:

> I went to China with Stewart the second time mostly to get the feeling of being there, and to hear China through Stewart's ears. I knew that he would be listening for any musical textures he could take away, and being a dedicated music appreciation student, I was interested to know what he would respond to and how those influences would come out in his voice. For my own part, I was going to have to find the essential truth in the story, and walking around villages like the one where LuLing grew up would give me an emotional sense I could work with.

STEWART:

> For our second trip I particularly wanted to see as many different kinds of Chinese opera as I could. Initially I wasn't so turned on by the idea of minority cultures, but then I found out that minority villages were often the only places you could find some of the old rituals we were interested in. I had no idea the extent to which the old culture had been decimated in the cities. Orville Schell had suggested that I see the film *Yellow Earth* to get a sense of the past, and he later told me, "What's so amazing about China is how rich their vernacular tradition once was, and how successfully they've killed it off."

AMY:

> One of my most vivid memories of that second China trip—this might sound a little risqué—was watching Stewart at work in the back room of a roadside restaurant surrounded by pornographic pictures. We had been talking about the opening restaurant scene all day on the bus, and when we finally got off to eat, the rest of us were all out front waiting for the food to arrive while Stewart hurried off to the back room to start composing underneath those posters of naked Western women. It was about as organic as you can get.

IV.

MUSICAL CHINA:
SACRED AND PROFANE

STEWART:

I think the single most powerful experience I had in China was the music we discovered at the village funerals on our second trip. My first reaction was, what is this Jewish kid from Texas doing in the middle of a very private ritual? Retroactively, it confirmed many of the choices I made and couldn't articulate at the time. Why did I think I needed two *suonas* in the Prologue? I don't know, but when we went to the funerals I immediately realized they were using the same instruments in the same configurations. I had no idea that percussion and *suona* were integral parts of life-cycle rituals. I just wrote to my ear.

AMY:

By the time I met up with Stewart on that second trip, he had already been through at least two funerals and his mind was already turning. When we'd walk through villages, he would get an idea and start humming something, and I was not only seeing the villages, but hearing the villages. Everywhere we went had a very specific kind of sound.

STEWART:

I'd been trying to find a character to balance Qian Yi—a male voice that was rough-hewn and clearly outside the Western operatic tradition. Then in Beijing we met Wu Tong at a party. He was singing his new version of *Blue Little Flower* and I thought, Jesus, what an amazing voice! And then I found out he played Chinese wind instruments! We later sat down with my music, and he explained that some of my writing for *suona* was "off the horn"—well, he didn't exactly use that phrase, but that's what he meant—and explained that there were special horns that could play the music as written, but the character of the sound would change quite a bit. So, of course, I revised it. The funny thing is, by the time I had my first lesson on the *suona* I'd already written about forty minutes of music.

Wu Tong:

Most of Stewart's music was not so difficult to play on the *suona*, and it fit the drama of the story as he explained it. He was obviously very bright and culturally sensitive to realize that much of the same music is played at both weddings and funerals. I could at least tell he was very kind, with an open heart and an open mind. He is not the normal classical composer. We talked about rock music and drank and smoked and sang Aerosmith songs, and I noticed a strong tension and excitement in the music—not East or West, but something in between. I have never seen a complete Western opera in my life, but his music goes in the same direction as much of the new music I play in the Silk Road Ensemble. Only the genre is different: a larger structure, a long plot line; one evening, one story.

Stewart:

The second time I met with Zhonghua, we fleshed out not just our working relationship, but also a good bit of the music. The way we'd work is, basically, he would show me things from his tradition and I would mess them up. And through that process we came to an understanding.

Zhonghua:

Before meeting Stewart, I had been thinking of how to break out of the whole set tradition of Peking Opera. I had worked with composer Guo Wenjing, who uses Western orchestration and a Western way of presenting music, but inside he is still very Chinese. All of the movements are traditional. With Stewart, it was a matter of completely destroying the tradition from within. Sometimes because of our language barrier I still don't always know what he wants to do, but I translate what I think he wants into music, and he seems to know what's happening.

STEWART:

During our sessions, Zhonghua pointed to his *daluo* and said, "Normally I play this on the beat. For you, I play off the beat." I think that speaks to the way we created our musical language. From the beginning I've tried to learn intuitively. I don't know anything about the tradition intellectually. I went and I listened. I worked with the musicians, and I wrote. Which I now realize is also the way Amy writes. We absorb the things that interest us, and somehow in the process it becomes part of the creative language.

V.

A NEW COLLABORATION

AMY:

I guess in most operas the writer finishes the libretto before the composer goes to work, but in our case the process was different from the very beginning. For me, the first thing I had to keep in mind was that no one ever sits down and reads a libretto for fun. Its function is similar to a screenplay in that it's there mostly to determine the overall structure of the piece.

STEWART:

I'm sure that writing the screenplay to *The Joy Luck Club* helped Amy in writing the opera libretto. She has a clear sense of the bare essentials in her stories, and a strategic way of moving a story through time, rather than simply on the page. The key thing is the way the ideas evolve, and words are only one way of doing that. Right from the beginning, Amy entered into the project with the idea that the music would tell the story. You wouldn't need to hear a single word to know what was going on. For her to let go of words is amazing, because words to a writer are what notes are to a composer.

AMY:

> Opera is definitely not my world. I get enough pats on the
> head elsewhere, and if I was going to be serious about doing some-
> thing like this, I couldn't have any ego invested in the project.
> Otherwise I wouldn't have been in the position to learn. I've loved
> wordplay ever since I was a little kid, so I never got tired of revis-
> ing things.

STEWART:

> One main advantage that the two of us had before we even started
> is that we both like to work in sequence. Librettist Michael Korie
> often likes to work on his scenes out of order, which I haven't done
> since *Where's Dick?* After that first opera with Michael, I waited till
> I had the complete libretto before I started writing music.

AMY:

> Stewart had several signature touches in his music that I already
> knew from his earlier pieces—the percussion, the repetition, the
> glissando in the voices—as well as a few new elements that I'd
> seen him pick up in China.

STEWART:

> We'd been just sitting around waiting for Michael to become avail-
> able when I finally said, "Amy, let's just start." She said, "I don't
> know what to do," and I said, "I know what to do, and you know
> what to write." So for the Prologue she sent me five or six pages
> structured as trios and solos, where each of the three women
> comes out and introduces herself in the most direct way possible.
> It was practically in Chinese opera fashion—like "Hello, I'm the
> apothecary. I've worked in this lousy place for three years."

AMY:

> In both novels and short stories, most writers tend to overwrite.
> For our process, I thought it was better to get everything on the
> page and then later cut back to the most essential, the most powerful.

As long as I'm working with someone who understands that, I'm happy to overwrite.

STEWART:

With music it's just the opposite. Composition is such a labor-intensive process that it's better not to write too much. With Amy, though, overwriting turned out to be a real bonus. Amy always had a certain level of trust in that she'd lay out a lot of stuff, hoping that I would choose things she was happy with too. Then we'd go back and forth. When I got her six-page draft for the Prologue, my first step was to cherry-pick through the text, keeping her order of ideas for the most part but sifting through to find the most musical and informational bits and leaving out the conversational parts. Out of six pages of Amy's wall-to-wall text, I sent back two pages of thin columns, ending with "I am like the village where I was born. Immortal Heart." Amy looked at my rather severe edit and wrote back, "Oh, so that's how it's done." And she never let me have control like that over her text again.

CHAPTER 2

HEART:

WRITING TO THE HEART

Even by the highly collaborative standards of opera, Amy Tan had a lot
of help with her first libretto, but not in the practical sense. No other
writers helped shape any given scene. Nor were any experienced librettists hovering over her shoulder, mentoring her in the craft. But from
the time she became involved in *The Bonesetter's Daughter* opera with
Stewart Wallace, Amy was surrounded by veterans from all corners of
the opera stage.

Perhaps the most liberating experience came in the initial creative meetings, where Amy found herself face-to-face with the broadest possible extremes in perspective: librettist and lyricist Michael Korie, Stewart's longtime writing partner, who came to the table with the utmost respect for the original story and its construction, and director Chen Shi-Zheng, who hadn't read the book, lest "Amy's original voice limit my conceptions of the story on stage."

Also in the mix was David Gockley, the newly appointed general director of the San Francisco Opera, who in his thirty-plus years at Houston Grand Opera had, in the words of the *New York Times*, "shaped the destiny of American opera." Gockley had shepherded no less than thirty-five world premieres, including two operas by Stewart and Michael.

Amy's most significant collaborator, of course, was the composer. Although she admits that at one point she knew so little about opera that she wasn't sure if the words or music came first, the writer who studied piano for fifteen years in her youth has called *The Bonesetter's Daughter* her "personal graduate course in libretto writing."

Two significant things happened during *The Bonesetter's Daughter*'s journey to the opera stage. First of all, it began to look and sound like the work of her collaborators. From the moment he entered the picture, Shi-Zheng started remaking the narrative in his own creative image. Working concurrently on *Monkey: Journey to the West*, an acrobat-driven "circus opera" with music by Damon Albarn and visuals by Jamie Hewlett, Shi-Zheng was looking for any excuse for acrobatic displays, from the surreally animated waiters in the opening restaurant scene to the floating bodies that would help lead Amy's story into the past.

The composer had his own distinctive approach. After culling the Prologue text from Amy's extensive notes, Stewart sat down regularly with his chief collaborator during their 2005 trip to China and discussed the opening scene in minute detail, honing the results line by line. It was not a working style that they could sustain in the real world—most of the time they lived on separate coasts—but it established a clear division of labor. In part because they shared a musical frame of reference in China, Amy was able to write acutely to Stewart's ear.

At the same time Amy's story was bending to fit her collaborators, it also began to reflect more of herself. After going some length to fictionalize true events in her novel, Amy and Stewart began searching for select images and compressions that could tell the story more directly. Soon LuLing would reveal her dementia not in the privacy of a doctor's office, as in the novel, but more dramatically in a restaurant during Chinese New Year, much as Amy's own mother's condition became obvious at a family Thanksgiving dinner. An episode from the book involving a trinket necklace becomes powerfully transformed into a mink coat, another iconic symbol drawn from Amy's life with her mother.

Stewart describes the Mink Coat Aria, which introduces Ruth's supremely complicated feelings toward her mother, as "the most conventional thing in the whole opera," but that hardly does justice to the writing. In Amy and Stewart's collective hands, a mink coat becomes a powerful visual symbol and a master stroke of narrative compression, reiterating themes (and quite a few words) from Amy's previous books in a rhapsodic summary of the writer's finer points concerning mother-daughter relationships.

1.

CHILDREN OF THE DRAGON

MICHAEL KORIE:

Before I met with Amy—I think even before Stewart had formally proposed making an opera to Amy—Stewart had asked me to read the book and see if I thought there was an opera in it. He has a way of finding unusual projects, and usually says, "Just read it before you say it can't be done." So I took it with me to a writer's colony and drafted an elaborate twenty-page synopsis, reorganizing the events of the book, picking through the ones I thought would work for an opera. Then I divided them into an epic opera in three acts, following the original structure of the novel.

AMY TAN:

The first time we all got together, Chen Shi-Zheng just sat there listening to us talk, and this quiet power of his started to unfurl. I described *The Bonesetter's Daughter* as a story about what needed to be remembered. There were three women of three generations: the daughter Ruth, a ghostwriter who has no voice of her own; her mother LuLing, who in a way also has no voice because she's not spoken her secrets to her daughter; and a ghost named Precious Auntie, who has no voice because her face was disfigured in a fire. Then, when Shi-Zheng started talking about how he could show all this on the stage, all the power of live theater started to hit me. You have to remember, I had no idea how operas are made. This was old hat for Stewart, but for me I saw the possibilities of another art form suddenly open up.

CHEN SHI-ZHENG:

My first thought was that the story needed a truly vast landscape. It opens in San Francisco as a touching mother-daughter story, but as it starts looking back to China it opens up into an epic. This is inherent in the story, and Amy's writing is already so sensual, with such a strong symbolic dimension that it practically becomes a myth. Much of the physical setting is autobiographical, but you know the Chinese like to say that we're all children of the dragon, and to me this makes her story link to all of us somehow. At first, I thought the treatment was too close to the novel, and the whole approach too close to musical theater. For this to be an opera, it needed some sort of abstraction. The first thing we had to do was to break the narrative from literal time so we could be free to float between the past and the future.

MICHAEL:

During our initial meeting, Shi-Zheng thought we needed to change the approach. He said the flow of events was too American for the subject matter, and more information should be delayed. Basically, he didn't always like knowing why something was happening at the time it happened. The essence of drama is always where, when, and how much you let out the backstory.

STEWART WALLACE:

Right from that first day, Shi-Zheng had put his thumbprint on the project, and everything we'd done was thrown up in the air. We had dragons swimming in fish tanks. And not just any dragons— Shi-Zheng had said, "These are not Chinatown dragons; they're Shun Lee dragons [named after a high-end Chinese restaurant across from Lincoln Center] manipulated by acrobats." The waiters would also be acrobats in continuous motion, and the whole scene would take on an abstract quality. The bonesetter could be the proprietor of the restaurant and function essentially as the storyteller. The ideas just flowed.

AMY:

I think what got to Shi-Zheng, and what he strongly conveyed to us right away, was to ask, "What's in our bones?" The personal always comes out of the epic, the historical, the mythical. So right away we started building to mythic. In the first act we got right to the marrow of our bones. We had images like the water on the lazy Susan in the opening restaurant scene that we could use to help amplify the story.

STEWART:

I had first approached David Gockley with Michael's and my original scenario, even before we met with Amy and Shi-Zheng. David, whom I've known for twenty years and who's been the single most important instigator of my large operatic works, came to one of our events in San Francisco and was convinced that the opera would be an epic. His first response was, "I don't want this to be six hours long." I told him I didn't want to write six hours of music, either.

AMY:

The novel is long, with many, many characters and subplots. We'd gone through about ten different versions trying to simplify them, and by the time we met with David we had a scenario that was pretty good. But he had some very good advice at that meeting: first, "simplify, simplify, simplify." The other was, "Make me cry." Both of these points I understood very well. Taking that advice along with what Shi-Zheng had to say, I knew there were many things in the story that could be communicated most effectively visually and musically. At that point the narrative path became less linear so that the other elements could deepen the story.

STEWART:

After that first meeting with David, we went back to the drawing board. With Shi-Zheng, we essentially blew the structure of the book out of the water. He'd ask, "What's this with the ink, the dragons, the blood?" He focused right away on the handful of images we needed to break the story down and start over. Right then we decided to open the opera with a dinner scene, with the fish tank and a lazy Susan as the two main scenic elements. We immediately called David again and told him we had an entirely different conception for the opera, and in a few days we flew back to San Francisco with images to show him. This happened in a week! The show as we had known it had been blown up and completely reassembled.

11.

A NEW DIRECTION

DAVID GOCKLEY:

Right away, I'd said the opera should be in two acts rather than three. I also remember suggesting that Ruth could also become her mother LuLing when we go into the flashback. After looking at the restaurant scene, I remember thinking that Ruth should have a scena—a real aria—at the end of the first act. There were various other tweaks and nips and tucks I suggested, some of which they actually took.

AMY:

What was great about the new structure was that it allowed for breakout moments where we could immediately see how the emotional moments would lead to one another. And it would allow for certain musical and textural motifs to evolve over time. We could see as we began to work through the opera that this structure would be a form that would allow for a lot of creativity while keeping the story very transparent.

MICHAEL:

Having a less structured libretto meant that the music would do most of the work, but I wasn't entirely comfortable with it. For one thing, with a novel this autobiographical, I just didn't grasp the story well enough to make these kinds of revisions myself. Also, at that point, Stewart only had a vague idea that he wanted to write American music using indigenous Chinese instruments. The sound of the music always affects the words I write, so this project was going to be a real challenge.

STEWART:

At that point, I was still thinking I'd incorporate a few Chinese elements the same way I'd used nonclassical sources in my previous operas. The orchestra in *Where's Dick?* was a giant electric band. So this was still going to be very much an American show.

MICHAEL:

The real problem, though, was that I knew they were planning a work trip to China, which came at a time when I was deeply involved with an opera of *The Grapes of Wrath* and the off-Broadway production of *Grey Gardens* moving to Broadway. I've traveled with Stewart before and I realize how important these trips are. When we were writing *Kabbalah*, we traveled in Israel for well over a month visiting several orthodox sects, visiting ancient ruins, and reading arcane texts that are only in libraries in Jerusalem. We simply couldn't have written that piece if we hadn't made that trip together. And since I was already going schizo moving between Broadway and another opera project, I had to get out of *The Bonesetter's Daughter* or else I'd be the one holding everyone back.

DAVID:

Stewart has had a long working relationship with Michael, who's a playwright in his own right and no wimp as a collaborator. *Harvey Milk*, in fact, was characterized as "an opera by Stewart Wallace *and* Michael Korie," not "an opera by Stewart Wallace with a libretto by Michael Korie." That's real distinction, which is to say that Stewart is used to working with strong partners. As far as working with Amy is concerned, he was already prepared for someone with a real spine.

AMY:

In some ways writing an opera libretto is similar to writing a screenplay, but they're also different in that, first and foremost, an opera is a live production, and secondly, the words are there to serve the music. Yes, you can say that it all starts with the story, and yes, there's a synchronicity in the words and music. Every time I sat down to write, I had to keep in mind that everything had to come together on a musical level. Every single word counts, and you can't have anything that's excessive. You can say that about screenplays, too, but the theater has many more elements involved—music, acting, singing, visuals. To me it's the most challenging kind of collaboration, but also the most rewarding.

STEWART:

What Amy and I didn't know at the beginning was that we have very similar ideas about language and rhythm.

AMY:

I use a lot of phatic words, which is a linguistic term for "filler," those fatuous phrases and verbal placeholders that normally in an opera libretto would be the first thing to go. But they can also help move the story along and reveal character. After Ruth has a dramatic moment of self-realization about how deeply her mother affects her—singing, "I won't ever kill myself. She'll kill me first"—her husband Art says, "I'll get the car." Why? Because that's what men say when they face an uncomfortable situation. What he says may not mean anything on the surface, but the words do mean something in another sense.

STEWART:

This was one way we could pack so many details efficiently. The first scene is an entirely different world from the Prologue, where the voices of Ruth, LuLing, and Precious Auntie intermingle and focus on character without advancing the story.

AMY:

About that Prologue, Stewart, I want you to know that the initial material I sent you were only notes for Michael Korie so that he'd know the kinds of things that were supposed to go in there. You immediately started criticizing my "libretto," and I want to make it absolutely clear right now that I never thought that was actually the libretto. Those were just my notes. I guess I should've made it clear that this was how I work; I just throw out a whole bunch of things at first, like verbal diarrhea.

STEWART:

Because Michael had become unavailable, I just automatically perceived your notes to be the real thing—or at least the first step toward the real thing. The reason I started sending you comments right away was that you had not just the essence but the entire structure of the scene already. But maybe you should've said something about those pages just being your notes.

AMY:

I did! I did! But you're a guy and didn't pay any attention. You're just like Art. At least I'm a little more like LuLing than Ruth.

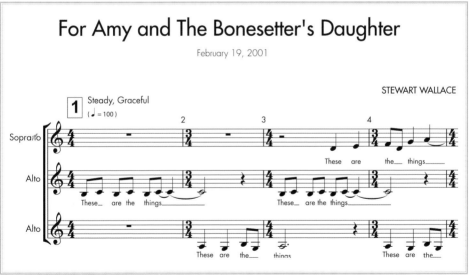

TOP *Amy and Stewart, from an early event for* The Bonesetter's Daughter *opera in San Francisco at the home of David and Emily Pottruck, with Amy's grandmother Gu Jianmei (c. 1905), pictured on the enlarged book jacket between them.*

ABOVE *Stewart composed a short piece for Amy's original publication party. The three voices, he later realized, contained the germ of an opera.*

ABOVE *To find the rural China of* The Bonesetter's Daughter, *Amy and Stewart left the over-developed east coast for a ten-day exploration of Hunan and Guizhou provinces, known for their large minority populations.* "*Minority villages were often the only places you could find some of the old rituals we were interested in,*" *Stewart says.*

OPPOSITE *Stewart and Amy in Dimen village, interacting with Dong villagers old and young on their research trip in 2005. Amy would frequently record their songs and play them back to the performers.*

Stewart pays the "tourist" price for a hulusi, a gourd wind instrument, in exchange for a free lesson (top left). Funeral music in Shanxi ranged from a contemplative Daoist ritual to the boisterous Hua Family Shawm Band. "Now I know what it feels like in a village," says Stewart. "There's a palpable sense of time and space and the way things move."

"I was particularly attracted to the roughness of Sichuan opera," says Stewart, who discovered full-length performances in a park in Chengdu (top). "These were not tourist shows, but an integral part of daily life." Stewart with a local male singer playing female roles (bottom).

"I was not a big fan of Chinese music," Amy admits. "Chinese opera I didn't understand at all. I had no idea who was good and who was evil." By the end of her first direct interaction with the art form, Amy realized that "all this music I thought was just empty ritual was very much alive with emotion and drama and tragedy." Amy strikes an operatic pose on stage in an old theater in Zhenyuan (top) and gets an extreme Peking Opera makeover (bottom).

Amy Tan's mother Daisy Chan (born Li Bingzi), the voice of The Bonesetter's Daughter *and the primary inspiration for her daughter's writing, seen here at age eighteen (top left), with daughter Amy (top right), and at age eight surrounded by her family in Hangzhou (bottom).*

111.

WRITING IN RESTAURANTS

STEWART:

Setting our first scene in a restaurant was an obvious idea, since that's where Jews and Chinese people have met for generations.

AMY:

Not only that. A restaurant is a usual gathering place where family members see each other whether they get along or not, whether their in-laws get along or not. It's also one of those settings—weddings and funerals being other examples—where the worst in people comes out. In my books, I've set several scenes at the Fountain Court, partly because it was my mother's favorite restaurant, but also because it was a noisy family place where anything could happen. It also seemed perfect for an opera, since it was conducive to a lot of action. Waiters could be dancing; fireworks could go off.

STEWART:

Strangely enough, Michael's original treatment had no restaurant scene. We'd put LuLing's "Alzheimer's moment" in a doctor's office, as it happens in the novel. Once Amy started working, we got rid of that scene in the doctor's office and eventually the flashbacks to Ruth's childhood, too. Once we had the restaurant for our opening scene, we decided that everything from the first part of the novel—right up through LuLing's O.J. Aria—would happen there.

MICHAEL:

Food was always a great impetus to get us started. Stewart always likes to meet at Balthazar. But when we looked again at that first scene, we decided the whole stage would be a lazy Susan like you find at a Chinese restaurant. I'd been thinking of a more structured outline, but this was a concept that could tell the story in a more postmodern way.

SHI-ZHENG:

Just to have everyone meet in a restaurant? How boring. But if the Chinese people are the children of the dragon, then anything is possible. It opens an entirely different world of space and reality. Your waiters can fly around the room and plop a pig's head on the table. Everything you think you know can be turned around. This scene set the stage for my whole approach, to take iconic Chinese elements and think of ways to transform them.

STEWART:

Shi-Zheng lets the restaurant unfold into an entire world. What made this idea particularly interesting is that Amy's mother had a very similar breakdown at a Thanksgiving dinner, so by compressing the events in the opera we wound up being much closer to reality.

AMY:

There are a lot of things in the opera that came from real life. This was just a matter of getting rid of unnecessary detail. What was key to me throughout the opera is that you always know intuitively what's happening just by listening and watching. So in that first scene we have a family in a restaurant. It looks like a happy gathering, but pretty soon you can see the tension, and eventually you can feel everything that's wrong in each of their relationships.

STEWART:

This was by far the hardest scene in the entire opera, because we had to introduce all the characters and immediately set the stage for everything that would follow. The family is celebrating both LuLing's birthday and Chinese New Year. We meet all the characters and then, in a single moment, everything falls apart.

AMY:

Clearly LuLing is losing her mind, yet on another level she can see everything that's going on. Everyone else, of course, simply thinks she's gone crazy and no longer makes sense.

STEWART:

> Amy was explicit that the first scene be funny, and it was immediately obvious to me that she thinks of humor the same way that I think about rhythm: as a device to get past the brain and disarm the audience so that they're open to whatever you have to give them.

AMY:

> Some people think of my books only as sensitive mother-daughter portrayals, but I always start with humor. Humor allows you to greet others with open arms, then by the time you get gut-wrenching, you've already got them. You can get away with anything because at that point people aren't going to resist. Early on, Arlene [Art's mother] says, "I like shellfish, it doesn't like me," and LuLing says, "So many things, they not like you." It's a funny exchange, but at the same time I have seemingly throwaway responses that show Ruth as being dismissive of herself and Art being controlling. These are examples of phatic phrases I was talking about: illuminations of character that have to come through as efficiently as possible, through what's said beneath the surface and then illuminated in the music.

STEWART:

> I think a lot of Amy's lines in that first scene are digs at my food allergies.

AMY:

> What do you mean? Even in the book I had Arlene being fussy. She couldn't eat this, couldn't eat that . . .

STEWART:

> Yes, but I really say, "My throat slams shut."

AMY:

> Really?

STEWART:

Maybe not "slams," but something like it. And not "it's a coffin for me." More like "nail in my coffin." But as you were saying, the words themselves are less important than the way the ideas evolve.

IV.
"SHE WANTED THE MINK"

STEWART:

One of the first things we decided about the opera is that LuLing would have to die. This wasn't originally in the book, but Amy had weaved so many details of her own life into the novel, particularly details and confrontations with her own mother, that when we started looking for powerful images that could efficiently convey what we needed in operatic terms, we began considering additional details from Amy's own life that weren't there before. In particular, there was Amy's mother wanting a mink coat, which we put right in the first scene.

AMY:

Sometime after *The Kitchen God's Wife* and *The Joy Luck Club* movie, my mother started hinting that she wanted a mink coat. I kept saying, "Why would you ever want a mink coat. First of all, you don't need it in California, and second, people won't like it." But she kept bringing it up, and I kept teasing her. Finally, I told her, "Choose whatever you want and I'll pay for it." But that wasn't the point. What she really wanted was shopping time with me. So we eventually went out looking for coats and she'd say, "This is for you later." I'd tell her I wouldn't wear a fur coat and would never buy one for myself. But I did try it on. That coat did mean something to her, because it was proof of my love. Despite what LuLing says in the libretto, my mother did want it, and she loved to show it off. Since she died, it's been in my closet in Sausalito. I think I wore it twice, just to think of her.

STEWART:

Musically, the Mink Coat Aria is the most conventional thing in the whole opera because it draws least from our experiences in China. This makes a point artistically by setting Ruth apart from the other characters. Throughout the opera, she stands in contrast to all these things around her because she has literally had no contact with them. Some of this I've only realized in retrospect, but the aria does introduce Ruth as having the least Chinese consciousness of any of the Chinese characters.

AMY:

Within this symbol of the mink coat we were trying to consolidate a lot of things from the book that had to do with relationships. The first were the mother's warnings, like "No running into street or you get squashed like sand dab. Both eyes stuck on one side of your head." And when Ruth would get quite spunky, her mother would say, "Maybe I kill myself right now." Ruth was obviously damaged, and we needed to collapse all of those feelings into just a few minutes of subtle shadings, where the nuance of emotion is a mélange of pain and rejection and anger and guilt.

STEWART:

What makes this aria particularly tricky is that it's about not being able to express the emotion you're trying to express. The scene is extremely convoluted in its emotional constipation, and what I tried to do is to aim at the striving and yearning embodied in it, but always leaving it unresolved and unsettled. It's very hard to find a way to express musically that she really loved her mother, but had no way to say it directly.

AMY:

It was a tough thing for me to write, too. And I understand how tough it probably was for Zheng Cao to sing it the first time. She sang it beautifully, but with no nuance. It was obviously an experience she didn't have. It has to be restrained, guilty, terrified—yet with a current of anger underneath. There was one phrase—"I wanna wear this dress"—that Zheng had sung in a pleading, sad voice. I told her, "No, it needs to be a confrontational, rebellious teenage voice."

STEWART:

That was my fault. I had told her to play it that way.

AMY:

Really? Well, it's not supposed to be like that. It's "I wanna WEAR. THIS. DRESS!" It's one of her first acts of rebellion against her mother, and she gets slapped in the face for it. Not literally, of course, but it's like the scene in *The Joy Luck Club* where the little chess champion throws a fit and tells her mother, "You wanna show off, then *you* play chess." Then, when she calms down and is ready to play chess again, her mother says, "You think it's so easy, so quick, so fast." And she loses all her ability to play chess, just like that. That's the feeling I wanted to capture. This aria had to take me back to that emotion, and the performance needs to find a way to get there. It's hard to transfer a complete emotional experience like that to someone else, but I remember the transformation that happened when Zheng was at my house. I showed her a picture of me at that age and told her, "This is the girl who's singing this line, and she's not whiny and pleading. She's a rebellious teenager, and gets smacked down." Then I brought out the mink coat, and suddenly it clicked. It all became real to her.

ZHENG CAO:

Stewart and I were at Amy's home working on the Mink Coat Aria in preparation for a development event at the San Francisco Opera. We were talking about the significance of the coat, and Amy got up and took it out of the closet. I was holding it in my arms and all of a sudden I *felt* it. It gave me goose bumps. At the event I sang to Amy, who came there playing her mother. I mean *my* mother. She was wearing the coat, and I swear I could still feel her mother's spirit in it.

V.

EMOTIONAL MOMENTS

AMY:

Besides providing the structure of the piece, a librettist needs to make sure that the music is authentic emotionally. Stewart was always looking for things to cut, and I had to make sure that he didn't get rid of any of the key elements. Throughout the entire project, David Gockley was "gas and breaks." Stewart was "search and destroy."

STEWART:

Come on, I would always preface my comments with, "Maybe this isn't a good idea. . . . "

AMY:

And I'd follow up with, "Stewart, what are you thinking? See your doctor. Eat more protein. You must be hungry. This is NOT a good idea." We had started writing the first scene when we were still on that second trip to China. We'd both be sitting in my hotel room and I'd write a few lines and give them to him right away. We'd go through line by line, and one of us would say, "This is too clumsy." Or, "The emotional state isn't right." We'd knock out a page or so in twenty minutes. And I could see he was composing when he first started reading the words. In my head I could see what was happening on the surface, and how the surface set the stage for something else. But when Stewart started talking about what was in his head, it was clear he already had a vision of what the music would be.

STEWART:

That was the only scene we wrote like that, trying to get a finished draft of the libretto before I composed. From there on, Amy would write with the idea that she was giving me more than I needed, and I would focus in on things I found important. Then the two of us would sit down with the music already written and

she'd respond to what I thought was important, or what it trig-
gered in me musically.

AMY:

I'd put in phrases and take them out until I found one that Stewart
liked. I don't mean I was trying to *please* him, in a subservient way.
I tried to find out what words he responded to on a musical level,
and pretty soon I was consciously writing words that comple-
mented his voice as a composer. Throughout the process, much of
what I was writing was determined by having heard the music
Stewart had written in the previous scene.

STEWART:

Also, Amy had an e-mail exchange with Michael Korie about what
elements she could use that would predictably provoke me.

AMY:

He said, the more disgusting it is, the more Stewart will like it.

STEWART:

Did you ever read Michael's libretto for *Hopper's Wife*?

AMY:

You probably gave it to me, but that was still during my phase when
I didn't get opera that much. And you also warned me not to study
other librettos too closely.

STEWART:

Michael wrote an aria for the painter Edward Hopper graphically
describing a porn film Hopper had just seen and how it inspired his
sense of color and texture.

AMY:

Was this relevant to the show? I mean, Hopper's paintings are so
controlled.

STEWART:

Oh, it was very relevant. We had intuited a dark side of Hopper from the paintings that didn't become public knowledge until a biography came out a couple of years later. The point is, once Michael read his lyrics, he was afraid of them. But I wrote what I thought was really beautiful music. This becomes particularly relevant to *Bonesetter's Daughter* by the time we get to Qian Yi's aria, with dramatic curses like "Leeches will suck your cock of all your slimy fluids."

AMY:

For that scene I just kept writing curses, trying to guess how you'd respond and what you'd choose.

STEWART:

And I kept all of it! Though I did have a hard time convincing my father that those words were really yours.

AMY:

I got a much clearer picture of what Stewart wanted once I started watching him work with singers. Stewart would guide them to sing in a particular way, with a very American diction. At first, I thought, jeez, he's so picky. But pretty soon I got to see exactly where he puts the emphasis in a phrase. Usually he wanted singers to articulate the ends of words that most people let fade. He just loves percussive consonants like *k*'s and *t*'s.

STEWART:

Most librettists, on the other hand, don't even know if their words will sing.

AMY:

From the time I first started writing fiction, I started reading things aloud, and if the prosody wasn't there I knew I had to change it. Maybe this was because I was raised by a mother who didn't speak English very well, but I've always been conscious of writing the kind of long phrases that singers might have trouble with. Once, we had a line that I thought had too many syllables. I said, "The word *opportunity* is hard to sing," but Stewart liked it and immediately sang it back to me. That was another bit of information I tucked into my bag of knowledge. Sometimes he liked surprising words interjected into lines that were otherwise rhythmically predictable.

STEWART:

One of the challenges of this opera was deciding when to opt for symmetry—which is a strong draw in Chinese culture—and when to break it. My natural tendency is to break it, and that's why I tend not to like text that is overly formal, or rhymed, because the line takes over the musical possibilities. Oftentimes, I would prefer to emphasize or break the rhythmic shape of a line through repetition.

AMY:

When it came to composing a scene, Stewart might say, "At this emotional moment, I think we need an aria." And the things we debated most back and forth were those emotional moments. Have we reached the exact moment when something should happen? Is there enough material setting it up? Or is there too much? Almost always, there would be too much. I think the process we'd developed helped us to deal efficiently with problems right as they occurred. In the first scene, for example, Stewart had cast Ruth's emotional state as mostly anger, while I had envisioned it as a sense of sorrow and regret. Whenever something wasn't working in the moment, we'd see what we could do to move it along.

STEWART:

The first time I tried to write the music for the restaurant scene, Amy said I'd gotten the music right for all of the characters except for LuLing, the story's mother figure. I didn't understand what was wrong, so she said, "LuLing is a person that people don't hear. Her in-laws would ask, 'You know what I mean?' and she says, 'I know you mean.'" Then I knew what she meant.

CHAPTER 3

CHANGE:

CREATING AND DESTROYING

A defining moment in Stewart Wallace and Amy Tan's collaboration took place in 2005 in a small town in Huangping county, Guizhou. Coming across a picturesque stone facade, the composer and writer entered a courtyard that, despite its surface disrepair, revealed an impressively ornamental interior carved mostly in wood. Noticing that the residents were busily involved in some sort of cottage industry, Stewart surveyed his surroundings with clear intent before motioning to Amy:

"Was that ink factory that burns down in the book made of wood or stone?"

Amy paused for a moment in disbelief. "Stewart, what do you want it to be?"

Thus did two opposing methods meet in stark relief: first, the outsider's reverence for the initial creation and, second, the original architect's willingness, even eagerness, to tear down that structure and rebuild from the ground up. Just as the destruction of the ink factory—a torrential eruption of fire and water, blood and ink—opens up the possibility of a new life for LuLing in Hong Kong and beyond, Amy's systematic purge of the story's novelistic trappings freed her characters to go their way on purely operatic terms.

Throughout their working process, no detail of the story was so hallowed that it went directly from novel to opera unfiltered. Whole characters were dropped (GaoLing, LuLing's sister in the novel, barely made it past the second treatment), and dramatic situations were compressed if not eliminated entirely. Several relationships became noticeably streamlined (notably, Ruth's upgrade from Art's girlfriend to wife). Key in these changes was the ease of conveying character and situation in a single sweep.

Although Amy often speaks of the artistic process in terms of intellectual interest, her work with Stewart first required reconsidering her story on an intuitive level, tracing it to its emotional core: Who, precisely, are these people? Where do they come from? Where do they go? From there, Amy's characters began their parallel journey on the opera stage.

What particularly distinguished their collaboration was that many narrative developments—not just in the music, but also in the libretto itself—didn't present themselves until after the creators had already started working. Writing each scene essentially in tandem before moving to the next meant that the libretto had no "early drafts." Some developments resulted from director Chen Shi-Zheng's simplified yet symmetrical approach, others from working directly with the cast. Qian Yi, for one, became an influence not just on Amy, who started looking for words that would particularly showcase her physical expressiveness, but also on Stewart, who would find that her *kunju* approach to his music would trigger significant changes in his composition.

Few cast members saw such dramatic developments in their roles as Hao Jiang Tian, the formidable bass singer playing Chang, the coffin maker. Having taken great joy in creating such a villain, Stewart and Amy had at least as much fun killing him off. Taking the principle of Chekhov's gun at face value, they framed Chang's climactic death in a way that LuLing's apprehension of marriage and fascination with knives in the first act became vividly explained in the second.

The collaborators faced a particular dilemma in dealing with Hong Kong. In both 2005 and 2006, Stewart and Amy scoured the city in search of vestiges of a 1950s Hong Kong that LuLing might have known, exploring Kowloon City fish markets by day and taking tram rides through the Western District at night. In the end, their preliminary scene at Victoria Peak, the exclusive enclave where LuLing had been employed by an expatriate family in the novel, wound up by necessity on the cutting room floor, leaving Hong Kong represented on stage solely by its iconic harbor, the spirit of the city told firsthand by its inhabitants.

In that way, Stewart and Amy managed to turn a well-worn cliché on its head. In *The Bonesetter's Daughter*, the city of Hong Kong is hardly "a character unto itself." Rather, it becomes a chorus.

1.

"NOT GUILTY"

AMY TAN:

When we were writing the mink coat scene, Stewart asked me at one point whether it was necessary to use the words *not guilty*. I told him, "Stewart, go ask your wife if she thinks *guilty* is the appropriate word." Partly, I know, it's the different sensibilities of men and women. Guys just don't have as much guilt. Maybe they'll try to prove to their fathers that they're young and capable. They may rebel. But for women, guilt is the nature of our relationships with our parents. It's not just a cultural thing. I used to think it was just Asians and Italians and Jews, but I've heard from German readers that guilt is a big thing for them, too. Saudi Arabians identify with it. It's an emotion that rings true in every mother-daughter relationship.

STEWART WALLACE:

In every single scene we have elements that don't simply push the story forward but elaborate connections in a number of ways between characters and even time frames. "Not Guilty" is one of those phrases that comes back again and again—particularly regarding O.J., although sometimes the phrases are only obliquely referred to.

AMY:

Stewart and I had already made a list of phrases that we used several times, and each time they came up we would change the context to either deepen or transform the meaning. Many of these phrases have musical elements within them, to the point that sometimes we don't even need the verbal phrase anymore. The scene where Precious Auntie kills Chang uses much of the same music as the O.J. Aria, but the treatment of the material is very different.

STEWART:

Even when the O.J. Aria first appears, it makes parallels between what LuLing saw with Precious Auntie and what she thought she saw with O.J. The family is sitting down to dinner and LuLing hears that her daughter Ruth is writing a book with one of the lawyers from the O.J. trial, and she says, "I know that story. I was there." She starts singing what is essentially a mad scene told through elements of Chinese opera: "That O.J. man he hide in bush waiting for his wife. I hiding there too, both of us waiting." So their dinner stops dead and becomes a moment in the bushes at a murder. On the surface, you realize LuLing is losing her grasp of reality, but she's also trying to tell her daughter something.

AMY:

> LuLing sees very clearly what's wrong with her daughter's relationship: Ruth has no voice. In her mind, LuLing talks to the dying Nicole and says, "If you my daughter, I warn you this: Watch your heart, watch out your husband. Save your life." LuLing looks at Ruth and it immediately becomes apparent that this is what she's really trying to tell her own daughter. This is a typical duality in the opera, of things being said one way and meaning another.

STEWART:

> Of course the people at dinner simply think she's gone crazy and no longer makes sense. It's a dramatic surface, but it later leads to the crux between the dramatic moment LuLing experienced with Precious Auntie and what she sees now with Ruth's marriage, both of which were absolutely true. Everything is tied up with guilt.

AMY:

> Many of LuLing's best lines come directly from things my own mother said. If you listen to LuLing in the first scene, she's clearly delusional, and yet everything she says about her daughter's marriage is entirely true. This was my mother. Throughout her life, she was immediately able to see through anything false. She had X-ray eyes in spotting false motives. She was a brilliant bullshit detector, and even when she was losing her mind at the end of her life, she was still a great bullshit detector.

* * *

AMY:

> For anyone who hasn't read the novel, I should probably say I was writing *Bonesetter's Daughter* at a time when my mother was losing her memory, and it's essentially a story about what needs to be remembered. It's about three women and the things they know are true.

STEWART:

The central character is Ruth, the American-born daughter, who essentially carries the story. She's the one who goes back in time to find the secret, which transforms her so that she becomes the mouthpiece for this story.

AMY:

As the role started to unfold, it became apparent that Ruth must become Young LuLing in China. There's an emotional reason for this, because I feel my life has been so informed by what happened to my mother when she was a young woman that it makes perfect sense dramatically for a young person to step in and become that older person to learn about the past. Ruth is very American, yet, there's this other part of her that when she goes back becomes very Chinese. She has an almost submissive American self—buoyant, yet innocent—while her Chinese self conveys a great sense of tragedy.

STEWART:

When we realized that Old LuLing was asserting herself into the past, we added an image at the end of the restaurant scene with her floating in her hospital gown. Ruth is becoming Young LuLing, but you can tell by the dress that the fit is not comfortable. Her uneasiness is also reinforced by having Old LuLing on stage. Amy went back to the first scene and introduced this idea where Ruth initially rebels against Art. LuLing balls her fist, then Ruth balls her fist. These ideas start to reinforce each other.

11.
EVIL, JOY, AND DESPERATION

AMY:

Every opera has to have a villain, and ours is Chang the Coffin Maker, a big, pompous braggart.

HAO JIANG TIAN:

> When Stewart first talked to me about the show I went out the next day and bought the book. But I didn't see much in it for me. There was this coffin maker Mr. Chang, and he did some bad things, but the character didn't seem to have a very big part. But Stewart said he had already written an aria for Chang, and for an opera singer to have an aria means you have a big role.

AMY:

> Even in the book, Chang had become the quintessential villain, but because we'd gotten rid of so many other characters, we just shifted all of the evil in the story onto Chang. I didn't mind whether or not any of this was true to the original novel, as long as we were true to what the story was about.

STEWART:

> I think the reason you capitulated so easily on these things was precisely because you thought we were doing something different from the novel.

AMY:

> I certainly didn't want to rehash the same things from the book. How boring! We'd already decided to have Chang himself, rather than Chang's son, marry LuLing. At that point, Michael Korie came up with the idea of having Chang actually be LuLing's father, which was strangely appropriate, since I already used that idea in *The Kitchen God's Wife*. The problem with having a purely evil character, though, is that there's little in the way of emotional shading. You get only one dimension.

TIAN:

> As a bass I'm usually typed into evil roles, but I tell you, I really like them. I even like the word *evil*. Whenever I play an evil person, I feel I understand the world a little better. I understand myself better. Inside everyone are some dark shadows. Maybe I can be a bit

selfish. Maybe I get jealous. Maybe I'll lash out at people at some point. Many people don't realize their dark side. Other people let it out indiscriminately. Either way can lead to tragedy.

AMY:

With Chang, I was able to shade the character only by playing with audience expectations. *When* is he going to be evil? In the scene where he's off to the side dictating a love letter to LuLing, you think, at first, maybe he's changed. Maybe he's seen some regret and is honestly dictating a love letter. Then through the music you hear that the very words that initially sound very innocent suddenly become twisted, and we start to play with the tension between what the audience already knows and what LuLing has yet to discover.

STEWART:

The thing we love about Chang, and what should definitely come out in the music, is what absolute pleasure he takes in his evilness. The utter joy he takes in doing horrible things to people makes him likable.

AMY:

Likable in the artistic, entertainment sense.

STEWART:

Well, yeah, you wouldn't want to have dinner with the guy. We were sitting around in Amy's house wondering, how should we kill him? And I said jokingly, "You should just cut his dick off."

AMY:

This was absolutely the perfect decision. I mean, if we just slit his throat, no one would ever remember that scene. Cut his dick off and no one will ever forget.

TIAN:

Is this really necessary, castrating me every night?

AMY:

I can already anticipate that some people will say it's a terrible thing, even more so because it's something a mother does for her daughter. But the truth is that there are people out there who do reach these points of desperation—and I'm not just talking about psychopaths and sociopaths. Normal people can reach levels of despair that lead to this kind of violence. We don't like to think of love being violent, and it's not about killing Chang as much as it is the extent to which Precious Auntie will go to help her daughter deal with a horrible evil.

STEWART:

In a way, the idea actually came from Shi-Zheng. When we had initially played him the O.J. Aria, he said, "It's good, but it's not enough. It has to happen again." Then Amy and I started trying to figure out what would be "enough," and when that "again" would be.

CHEN SHI-ZHENG:

When I first heard the O.J. Aria, I told Stewart, "Give us a reason for this music to come back." This is a story about ghosts, and ghosts never really go away. In this story we have to hear how our characters come to terms with their past.

TIAN:

Anyone who lived through the Cultural Revolution has a mark inside them that will stay forever. From the time I was able to come to the West, I could see life from many angles. Playing a character like Chang you suddenly realize, wait, I've had these thoughts before myself. Sometimes you didn't realize there was a bad seed planted in you just waiting to sprout. We Chinese, especially my generation and a little older, have a culture of keeping everything inside. When you find a window to let those feelings out, you gain the energy to move forward.

AMY:

Our biggest question in that scene was who would participate in the killing. Would it be Old LuLing or Young LuLing—meaning Ruth—who helps Precious Auntie? We decided to involve Young LuLing, so that Ruth can fully understand her mother's trauma and experience firsthand exactly what Precious Auntie did for her. People are going to think that I do hate men, but the scene was so heightened emotionally and Chang just so evil that he deserved that kind of prolonged agony.

111.
"LOOK AT THESE HANDS"

STEWART:

Amy had always maintained that the grandmother, Precious Auntie, is the keeper of the family secrets, and to my mind she was also the voice of tradition in the story. Having seen Qian Yi play a ghost in Chen Shi-Zheng's nineteen-hour *Peony Pavilion*, I instantly saw the power inherent in having a Chinese opera singer play the grandmother. The idea took shape in the narrative, and likewise the narrative was shaped by her as a performer. That didn't affect me so much musically at first, because I didn't really know what that meant. I hadn't worked with her directly until I started teaching her the music from the Prologue. But I thought whatever I wrote could possibly evolve into something related to her *kunju* training.

AMY:

As soon as I knew that Qian Yi would be playing Precious Auntie, I started keeping in mind things that might be amenable to gestures, the kind of lyrics like "I make my hands into a bowl" that might lead to something that she could do with her hands.

STEWART:

One of the reasons hand gestures were so important is that initially we weren't entirely sure of how we were going to resolve the fact that Precious Auntie doesn't speak. In the book, she only grunts and gestures. Obviously we're writing an opera, and we were going to resolve it with her singing, but the initial reason Qian Yi became our choice for the role was her strong gestural language. From that grew other choices, in terms of both the sounds of words and the way they were used.

AMY:

It wasn't just gestures with her hands, I should add. I started thinking of all kinds of things that would be conducive to body movements. At one point she's on her stomach as a worm, for example. Even though her character isn't supposed to be able to speak, I think of all the singers she had the most effect on the actual libretto.

STEWART:

I remember writing something in my initial notes about "speech-song with percussion," but I didn't get around to working with her on that until after I'd written the Prologue. When we started working together, she'd struggle with a particular phrase, or it wouldn't sound quite right, so after a while I'd say, "Why don't you try to sing it like Chinese opera." Then she'd take another pass at it, and from there we would shape it. I wasn't just saying, "Sing this in *kunju*." It was more like, "Show me what you would do." Then I'd start saying, "Keep this." "Change this." "Bring this part up." "Take this part down." We'd work everything out musically, as if I were composing for her, except that we did it in real time.

QIAN YI:

When I do traditional opera, I can perform nineteen hours with no sweat, but after five minutes with Stewart I start looking for excuses to stop. Drink some water. Throw open the windows. I have to think a lot. In traditional opera, you just do one episode, then move to the next. Certain parts of my brain can rest. But if I have to do movement and singing *and* speak in English, I have to use my whole brain. I have to think about everything from the beginning, and I can never fall back on anything I already know. Sometimes I could see what Stewart and I were doing and I thought, wow, this is really good. But other times I didn't even recognize myself anymore.

STEWART:

QianYi and I tried many exercises so that we could figure out how the English language might intersect with her *kunju* technique, and after a while I realized that it all boiled down to language. At that point, I'd ask her to sing something happy, then something sad, then something crazy—all in her original language. Then I asked her first to sound the words for me so that I could understand their relationship to the music.

QIAN YI:

Stewart can be so intimidating. He never let me get away with anything. But he really does know how to use actors well. He's not like several other composers I've worked with, who just ask me, "Sing something *kunju*." That kind of thing drives me crazy. Just think of the line, "My name is Precious Auntie." There are literally hundreds of ways to sing that one line, and each way will express something a little different. Stewart has a very clear idea of what his music should sound like. He's very detail-oriented. Sure, there are times that I put a little twist and he'll say, "Keep that." But he is very solid in what he wants, and that's what gives me the room I need to play around.

IV.

"STUCK IN HONG KONG"

STEWART:

> What interested us in Hong Kong in terms of the opera was its literal and spiritual position as a place of transit between the Old World and the New, which we also relate to as the basis for the entire American experience. Hong Kong also has a similar verticality and sense of space to Manhattan, so as a New Yorker, I felt I could immediately relate to the city.

AMY:

> Dramatically, the reason for setting a scene in Hong Kong is to explain the gap in LuLing's life. Obviously she's older by the time she gets to America, and somehow she's become self-sufficient, but we needed a context for us to see how she's survived emotionally. One of the things that's always impressed me about Hong Kong is that everywhere you turn, you see people who've found a way to carve out their niche, and that is exactly how I saw LuLing. While still being true to the part of her that comes from an ink-making family, she reinvents herself in the company of people in need of a voice. By using the ink she has with her to write letters for women whose husbands had gone to America, she gives them what they need—and also manages to comment about herself through the letters she writes for other people.

STEWART:

> I know at some point we said "no writing on stage" because it's always dreadful dramatically. We'd meant that as a way to open up more inventive possibilities for shifting the setting from San Francisco to China than just having Ruth find LuLing's memoir, as she does in the novel. The way that Amy has LuLing earn money essentially as a ghostwriter for these other women also makes LuLing become that much closer to Ruth.

AMY:

We don't have Precious Auntie showing LuLing how to write with
the ink, which was in the book, but, yes, I'd had these kinds of
similarities across all three generations. All three women are writers of a sort, but none of them writes for herself. Actually, the
idea of LuLing being a letter writer in the opera came from one
of the books I'd started and threw away between *The Joy Luck Club*
and *The Kitchen God's Wife*. Only in that book, my scribe was a
woman disguised as a man writing letters for the illiterate workers in San Francisco's Chinatown. I think I only wrote about thirty
pages, but the idea resonated heavily with me because when my
father first left my mother to come to the U.S. he wasn't entirely
certain he was going to have her join him. Finally, she wrote her
husband a letter—I say "husband" because they called themselves
husband and wife even though they weren't legally married—and
he had her join him. As I was writing this scene, it made me think
about the whole emotional impact of what my mother went
through at that time.

STEWART:

Another reason Hong Kong seems familiar is because of the movies,
both those from Hollywood and those made there. Hong Kong
films in particular capture a vibrancy on the streets that sometimes
makes Manhattan seem like a tiny fishing village.

AMY:

Visually, one of my strongest impressions of Hong Kong has always
been seeing people gathered by the harbor. Sometimes you can
sense their desperation. The city moves so fast that you often don't
know which way to turn. Our chorus shows people of all ages and
backgrounds singing, "I'm stuck in Hong Kong." There's an obvious
irony in setting this scene in the 1940s, because everybody today
knows how successful Hong Kong has become, but it wasn't so
obvious back then. I was tempted to play up the irony and have
some of the chorus members step out and tell us how they

eventually become successful, but after a while we decided that reduction would make the scene more powerful. And after we'd been to Hong Kong, that idea seemed a bit too obvious.

STEWART:

After spending a couple of days seeing historic Hong Kong, both colonial and Chinese, the only part of the territory we wound up using was the harbor. Amy had originally planned to include a scene at the Peak, but after we opened Act II at the harbor we all realized that the Peak would be an unnecessary diversion, as well as a complicated set change that made no dramatic sense.

AMY:

Unfortunately, one of my great memories of our stay in Hong Kong was going to the fish market in Kowloon City, which also had such a wonderful cross section of people. I originally wanted to include the market, because that smell is usually what I think of when I think of Hong Kong. But I'm comfortable using only the harbor. It's a truly iconic image, and so wonderfully open and spacious. And when most people think of Hong Kong, they first think of the harbor.

STEWART:

You also think of rain, which fills many of my cinematic memories of Hong Kong in films like *The World of Suzie Wong*. For the opera, we have a rainstorm that works as metaphor. As I read the libretto, I could almost hear Amy saying, "Stewart, you and Shi-Zheng want water? I'll give you water!"

AMY:

The storm was the perfect way to introduce Chang in Hong Kong. We thought he would become more sinister in the scene if LuLing first meets him as possibly some sweet man who just wants to write a love letter. As the letter goes on, it becomes more and more perverse. If you see the whole scene, it has perverse overtones from the start, but we wanted to illustrate the emotional complexity that even in beautiful things there can be something twisted and ugly. We wanted to play up that duality, at the same time trying to get the audience to wonder when LuLing would discover it for herself.

V.
A GROWING COLLABORATION

AMY:

I do think that one reason I was able to get up to speed as a librettist so quickly was because of the process I'd already undergone in writing the screenplay for the movie of *The Joy Luck Club*. Looking back, I see that director Wayne Wang and my co-screenwriter Ron Bass were both much more protective of the original story than I was. I would always be the one saying, "You know, in terms of our time frame and the context, I don't think this scene is necessary." I was always the one cutting.

STEWART:

By the time we got around to writing the scene in the ink studio, Amy had changed the whole backstory. Suddenly there's no Baby Uncle, no family, no concubines. Now they were all just slaves. I asked her, "Wait, how can we lose all that?" I was invested in that story by that time. It had the dynamic of a real family relationship. But Amy would just say, "Too complicated to explain. Not necessary."

AMY:

Actually, that sounds like my mother: "Too complicated. We do this way." But do you know how much time it would've taken to explain all that? And it did nothing for what we were trying to accomplish. I had a hard enough time fitting it all in the novel.

STEWART:

Getting the story to the bare essentials on stage, we both added and took out so much that if you use the novel as your guide, or look at the libretto on a literal level, the story obviously has a few gaps.

AMY:

There's the matter of Ruth and Art. Do we want to show ambiguity in the relationship? Absolutely. On one level, Art is there to show what kind of shape Ruth was in at the beginning of the opera. But there should be an obvious attraction between the two of them.

STEWART:

Our decision not to closely follow the novel opened up the possibilities for many elements that don't simply push the story forward but manage to elaborate on it in a number of ways. There are lots of references that come back again and again, even if they're referred to only obliquely at certain points.

AMY:

I love double entendres. In everything I write, I look for opportunities to use certain phrases that can be transformed in some way by using them in different contexts. My notebooks for the opera are filled with examples like "genuine," "longest lasting," or "words that never fade."

STEWART:

At the opening of Act II, Amy writes, "My fate has changed." These themes of fate and luck and hope and destiny are very much the essence of her writing style in general. She works very much like a composer, laying out themes and playing around with them, frequently turning them on their head.

AMY:

As an artist, you make up these things for your own intellectual interest. It's only supposed to be meaningful for you at the time, and you're the only one who needs to know how it fits into the process. As a reader or listener, you don't need any of this to follow the story. One probably *shouldn't* be aware of any of this while you're in the story. But if you go back and listen again, you'll find that particular phrases, whether musical or textural, often reemerge in very different contexts.

STEWART:

Many of these twists revealed themselves only as we went along. On one level, we always knew where we were going in the show, but the lack of literal, direct translation from Amy's book opened new doors to finding other images or situations that were more powerful. Once we came up with the idea of Precious Auntie being the bridge through which Ruth and LuLing could pass, the element of time travel opened up an entirely new way into the story. Organically, the story could flow back and forth at the same pace, with revelations from both the past and the present happening at the same time.

AMY:

Stewart and I had made a list of phrases that we use repeatedly. The first time around, you can grasp the emotional state on the surface immediately, but once that phrase comes back you need to see how it had warped. Many of these phrases have musical elements deeply embedded within them, to the point that sometimes we don't even need the verbal phrase anymore. The scene where Precious Auntie kills Chang uses much of the same music as the O.J. Aria, but the treatment of the material is very different.

STEWART:

Over time, we would have the whole shape, the entire context. I would respond to Amy's words, and the music that I wrote would affect what she wrote next. In that way, the screw kept getting tightened.

CHAPTER 4

CHARACTER:

BUILDING THE BONES
OF AN OPERA

In light of Amy Tan's love of wordplay, it's particularly appropriate that the Chinese character for *character* also means "bone." She and Stewart Wallace spent countless hours pondering multiple meanings of the same word, or seeing how a single word can subtly shift in meaning with a change in context, so their discussions about the "character" of their opera ranged widely depending on the circumstances.

How is one to define the essence of *The Bonesetter's Daughter?* The author first found her inspiration in the dragon bones that have captured the Chinese imagination for centuries, but that was hardly the first time that bones have appeared in her work. The composer, for his part, has long found personal resonance with her more characteristic use of bones as a symbol for the core of human nature. Within this definition, heritage and destiny are but two sides of the same coin.

The initial challenge for director Chen Shi-Zheng was to represent those picturesque metaphors from the page in strictly visual terms. Although he was as eager as Amy and Stewart to avoid a traditional linear narrative, Shi-Zheng's approach was modeled not on the archaeological layering of his collaborators but rather on the layering of contemporary media.

Beyond that, Stewart and Amy had matters of casting to consider. Both were preoccupied for different reasons with finding the right singer to play Ruth, the American-born daughter and central role in the story. Next in their priorities was finding LuLing, the immigrant mother, who shows clear signs of dementia as the story begins. Stewart's concerns were primarily musical; whoever played Ruth would be on stage for most of the opera. Amy's priorities were for the most part emotional: *The Bonesetter's Daughter* was a mother-daughter story with details taken from her own life, and as exacting as Stewart could be with his music, Amy was similarly demanding of the singers' expressive qualities. Stewart and Amy agreed heartily on Zheng Cao, a singer of great emotional range, to play Ruth. In looking for someone to sing the role of LuLing, Stewart found in Ning Liang a source of charm and exasperation worthy of Amy's own mother.

For two mezzo-sopranos who both claim *Madame Butterfly*'s Suzuki as a signature role, the lyrical Zheng and the chocolate-rich Ning could not have more different voices, or more contrasting personalities. With the story and the cast mostly in place, Stewart began composing his music with one ear trained on his singers and one eye focused on his librettist.

From the time that *The Bonesetter's Daughter* began its journey as an opera, the medium itself altered the very question of what makes up the story's character. For Stewart, finding the right sound world for Amy's characters was the fundamental aspect of the journey. This being an opera, the composer's approach was largely rooted in verbal language, particularly in establishing a musical vocabulary that would reflect the essence of characters who didn't grow up speaking English. That said, both Stewart and his singers were not afraid to point out the irony that getting the desired musical result was anything but effortless.

Even on a nonverbal level, Stewart's extensive work with Peking Opera percussionist Li Zhonghua and *kunju* performer Qian Yi—both of them willingly pushing beyond the constraints of their own traditions—yielded a world that contained palpable elements of both China and the West without being fully beholden to one side or the other. It was an approach that was fully in keeping with Stewart's nature as a composer, and yet entirely in character with Amy's story.

1.
STAGING LITERARY METAPHORS

AMY TAN:

One of themes I keep returning to in my work is that of bones. What do we have in our *bones*, meaning what is it that's passed from generation to generation? I'm not sure exactly how frequently it turns up in my work. I haven't done a "bone count"—there are some things you don't want to analyze too much as a writer—but bones are one of the images that I do tend to reiterate.

STEWART WALLACE:

That sort of ideal in Amy's novel *The Bonesetter's Daughter* was also something I had found in *Harvey Milk*: not just that you carry your history in your bones, but that you have the chance to make your own history by connecting with your past. Personal history transcends shame. Those feelings are palpable in the novel, but I've found they can be even more powerful on stage.

CHEN SHI-ZHENG:

Amy's writing has a lot of metaphors. The problem when we get to the stage is that there are so many symbols that you have to sort through them all to figure out what the story is about visually. You have to find the essentials, what you want people to take home. I usually like to focus on the simplest iconic elements in a way that turns cliché into myth.

AMY:

The impetus for the *Bonesetter* novel had been the idea of dragon bones, which came by chance when I met the head of the Chinese archaeological team who discovered Peking Man. I was writing *The Hundred Secret Senses* and doing research on caves. This was the early 1990s and you couldn't just Google something back then— you actually had to go look for it. So I was exploring the caves in Guilin when I got an invitation to go to a dinner honoring this archaeologist, who was almost a hundred years old at the time. I took it as a sign that I should write about it somewhere, even though I didn't have room for it in my novel then.

STEWART:

We had thought of the opera in archaeological terms. The structure, though it appears on the surface to be a linear narrative, is made in emotional layers, like the layers of history in an archaeological dig. So even though we got rid of most of the overt references, parts of it still lay beneath the surface.

SHI-ZHENG:

Linear narratives are not the only way to tell a story. The Chinese opera I grew up with never reflected physical reality, so I was interested in finding an expressive way to approach the material not bound by physical laws. There are so many possibilities inherent in this story that my job is to make it all transparent. This approach has become an obsession with me, because so much in the world was always hidden when I was growing up. You were never allowed to go to very many places.

AMY:

What struck me about the nature of archaeology, particularly when you talk about discovering the oldest human beings, is that the theme could resonate in fiction, in large part because it resonates in my life. You uncover the past by sifting through layers of things that otherwise seem meaningless. You encounter broken bones that were once part of people, lives that never got repaired. Peking Man, you remember, was the partial remains of many bodies, and the first of the remains found was from a woman. Emotionally this idea struck me as both a part of my life and a part of my fiction.

SHI-ZHENG:

In fiction, Amy thinks in terms of archaeological layers; on stage, I think of different time frames. I had just directed my first film, *Dark Matter*, and was still fascinated with the possibilities of manipulating time—going backward, fast-forward, changing speeds. I've always been conscious of how you need to move some things faster or slower for them to register in our normal vision, and early on in *The Bonesetter's Daughter* I had intended to incorporate video projections to give us the freedom to bounce between worlds. If our kids are able to do that on a computer, why can't we do that on stage?

STEWART:

We had many ideas along the way. We had a "bone chorus" at one point. We thought about the chorus coming together to make a giant Peking Man on stage at the end. We'd even talked about using one of Amy's bits about the first human word ever spoken being *ma*, and I was going to have the sound of *maaaaaaaa* like some kind of low Tuvan throat singing. But all that is gone now.

AMY:

We also have ink on stage, which was also a recurring image in the novel. There's a particular passage in the novel where a writer is describing to LuLing a book of brush paintings called *The Four Manifestations of Beauty*. The four are "Competence," "Magnificent," "Divine," and "Effortless." This all came from my friend Bill Wu's description of the calligraphy of C. C. Wang. Bill was an expert in Asian art, as well as my cultural mentor in all things Chinese—the intersection of art, music, poetry, architecture, gardening, and food into one aesthetic that was "the Chinese mind." I'm still mourning Bill, who died of a heart attack last December in the Shanghai airport. He taught me so much about Chinese culture.

SHI-ZHENG:

The way that Stewart and Amy treat the story is both eccentric and eclectic. Normally, the music in an opera provides emotional depth, but here it also provides symbolism, which opens itself to visual elements. It offers many possibilities in creating dreams, whether you're using video projections or live dancers. The story is not driven by any one medium, which I think is a very Chinese thing. In the Chinese mind, the person who can integrate the most elements in his life and work is the greatest master.

STEWART:

Shi-Zheng kept complaining that we had too much: the dragon, the ink, the writing, the blood, the bones. I don't know that he succeeded in cutting anything out. They're basically all still there, although the ink has now taken on a subsidiary role. Precious Auntie was originally going to kill herself by drinking a ladle of boiling ink. Now she uses the dragon bone, which is also the instrument of Chang's death and a much more powerful symbol. The ink has retreated in the background, although the black rain we'd planned for the end of Act I is still there. Shi-Zheng's plan is for the rain to mark Chang, which will make the symbolism of the ink palpable. The village will be portrayed as a kind of ink-brush painting, and Shi-Zheng has also talked about having a virtual waterfall of ink that will continue to be projected throughout the wedding. Shi-Zheng's approach connects all these images so that nothing is merely decorative or illustrative. Everything is essential. He's pushed us in that direction too, particularly regarding structure. We've constructed both the libretto and the music so that nothing is wasted.

11.

FINDING RUTH AND LULING

STEWART:

The central character in the opera is Ruth, the American-born daughter, which is a very difficult role to cast because she bears the weight of the entire story on her shoulders. Obviously, when we started looking for someone we were thinking about the voices, but vocal quality was only one factor. We also had to consider the strength of character and personality. Whoever plays Ruth has to be on stage for most of the opera.

AMY:

Stewart and I had many discussions about who should play Ruth. I strongly believed she needed to be American—to sound and act fully American, especially at the beginning—because after she goes to China she's transformed and becomes the mouthpiece for the story.

STEWART:

Amy was particularly adamant about this after she heard the demo recording we made of the Prologue—this was a central plot point, after all—and I was scared that a nonnative speaker playing Ruth would sound like José Carreras singing *West Side Story*. Also, I'd originally conceived of the role for a soprano, so mezzo-soprano Zheng Cao had two strikes against her from the beginning. But David Gockley was insistent that I meet her. He forwarded me a recording of her singing one of Jake Heggie's songs in beautifully idiomatic American English, and said, "If you really need a soprano, we'll get a soprano, but you should at least hear her."

ZHENG CAO:

David Gockley first told me about the possibility of an opera based on *The Bonesetter's Daughter* back in 2004 when he was still general director of the Houston Grand Opera and I was there singing Daniel Catan's *Salsipuedes*. I immediately read the book and decided I wanted to play Precious Auntie. It was such a heroic character that I couldn't believe anybody wouldn't want to play Precious Auntie. But I don't think David thought I was serious. He said, "But she's so old. . . ." And I said, "No, she's not. She died young. She comes back as a ghost." I mean, how great is that? But even then, David was already thinking of me as Ruth.

STEWART:

I heard Zheng sing Rosina in *The Barber of Seville* in Louisville, Kentucky, and frankly, it didn't do much for me. Not that she didn't sing well, but nothing in her performance spoke to the qualities we were looking for in Ruth. But Zheng and I went back and rehearsed the Prologue in her hotel room, going through her part line by line, seeing how many ways she could make each sound.

ZHENG:

Soon after, I got an e-mail from David telling me that they wanted me for the part, he invited me to go to a play based on Amy Tan's story "Immortal Heart," which later became part of *Bonesetter's Daughter*. We went, and there in the audience was Amy Tan! You have to realize, after I read *Bonesetter's Daughter* I swore I'd read all her books as soon as I could, but I never got around to it. So that night, all I could say was, "I haven't read all your books!" She smiled and shook my hand and said, "I'm so happy you're going to be our Ruth." I was still a little shaken and blurted out, "I've never done a live character before. All my other characters have been dead." All the time I kept thinking, oh God, why am I saying these things?

AMY:

> David Gockley came to a performance at Word for Word, a San Francisco theater company that was doing a play based on a story of mine that had run in the *New Yorker*. He had a mezzo-soprano with him named Zheng Cao, who was originally from Shanghai but had been living in San Francisco for some time. Her English was amazingly good, though she still had a bit of an accent. But she was so effervescent and emotive that I was convinced she could do anything.

STEWART:

> One of the great things about Zheng was that she could tolerate my working process. She also enjoyed doing whatever I asked her to do, which is pretty unusual for a singer. Of our three women principals, I associate her most with the standard repertory—probably because I first heard her sing Rossini—which makes her thoroughly appropriate to the role of Ruth. But she turned out to be surprisingly flexible in her interpretation and the kind of sounds she could make.

ZHENG:

> When I was seven years old I almost got picked to be a Peking Opera singer, and I was crushed—crushed!—that I didn't get past the finals. I'd made it all the way to the last round—even as a little girl I had a very loud voice—but at the time I was either too large or too small, I don't remember. Life had a different destiny for me. By the time I got to the Shanghai Conservatory they put me in the Western vocal department because they said my voice is not for Chinese folk music. At the time, when I was diving into Western music, I thought, why would I ever want to learn Peking Opera? Now I'm embarrassed to say I don't know it at all.

NING LIANG:

> You know, I'm still a little embarrassed because the first thing I said to Stewart when I met him at lunch was "I don't play old women." At that time I didn't know anything about him or his

music. But the way he explained the opera sounded fascinating. A few days later he asked me to sing at a fundraising event in Hong Kong, and I told him I could have two of my students sing the other two parts. So they all came to my empty new apartment and we rehearsed his Prologue. He had me sing LuLing and then Precious Auntie.

STEWART:

When I first met Ning I thought, what a diva, and potentially a pain in the ass. But I quickly warmed up to her, partly because she works so damned hard. Working with Ning a few days later, I saw how diligent she was and, frankly, how generous she was with her students. It was a completely different side of her. So adorable and sweet and kind. At that point I thought, here's our mother.

NING:

Stewart later showed me a picture of Amy's mother and said, "Ning, you know Amy's mom was the most beautiful person in her family." I said, "Doesn't matter, she's still an old lady." But then he told me a little more about Amy's mother, and when we looked at the O.J. Aria, he explained that it was something the character sings at the end of her life, that it was inspired by Amy's own mother when they found out she was experiencing Alzheimer's, and the person performing has to sing crazy. So I get this picture in my mind of being confused and not knowing where I am. I realized this would be a real challenge.

ZHENG:

When I was at the Shanghai Conservatory in the mid-1980s, Ning Liang had just graduated and was already an accomplished singer. She was one of the first Chinese singers to win international competitions, and she'd already left for graduate school at Juilliard. I looked up to her, you know. We all did. She was the singer that we all wanted to be. When I was seventeen, she was already my idol.

STEWART:

What's so unusual musically about Ning is the quality of her voice. She has this "chocolate bottom"—a contralto depth, though with the high range of a true mezzo. What blew me away was when she came to New York to record a demo of the Prologue. Of the three women we used—Zheng wasn't involved yet—Ning was easily the best equipped for what we needed, and the most efficient in the studio.

NING:

I can't imagine any singer who wouldn't want to work with a composer. Most of the time we only get to work with a conductor, which means everything is secondhand already. Maybe you sing a new production—that's better. Once someone has already done the role, you're just following in her footsteps. Literally, you have to stand in the same position because of the lighting. But you can always discuss a new production with the director. Your opinion helps shape the results. If you're lucky, you can sing a new opera and have the composer right beside you. You can say, "These notes aren't comfortable." Or, "The volume is too loud here." Stewart was always happy to change a few notes.

STEWART:

If you compare what Ning sings in the Prologue with what she sings in the O.J. Aria, you'll see a profound difference in the music. I wrote the Prologue from a generic musical idea, with no specific singer in mind. I had no idea how well those low notes would resonate in her voice. When I heard that "chocolate bottom," I came to the O.J. Aria with a very specific voice in my ear. I began thinking of ways to target both the low and the high points in her range. When she sings those low Fs and Gs, it's terrifying, yet hauntingly beautiful.

NING:

Much of contemporary music today can be very harsh. You hear the characters singing about love and you think, "Ai! That's supposed to be love?" But Stewart not only has imagined the story in the music, but *feels* how it can be told. He writes melodies that you can remember, which is pretty rare today. And the music is dramatic. The vocal range alone is pretty dramatic. He digs in to the extremes. But somehow it doesn't feel extreme because it all falls within my technique.

111.
MOTHERS AND
DAUGHTERS, FOR REAL

AMY:

My mother often threatened to kill herself, and I was always on the verge of saying, "Well, just do it, then." Later, I learned to laugh about it. My mother and I would talk about those things, and there was no shame for either of us. Also, she had no problem reading her own words when I started writing my fictional conflicts between mothers and daughters. There was never, "How could you tell everyone such private family things?" It was more like, "Why don't you tell them about the time I crashed the car?" There was no shame. She got great joy out of it. Somehow for her, instead of being tragic, it became heroic.

STEWART:

By the time I met Amy's mother she had already been diagnosed with Alzheimer's. I remember a dinner at the Fountain Court and also a gathering at Amy's house during rehearsals for *Harvey Milk* where she was clearly fading in and out during the evening. Interestingly enough, it was music for LuLing, the story's mother figure, that I had the most trouble writing in the opening scene. I'd punched her lines hard in the music, and Amy later told me to back off. She said, "LuLing is a person that people don't hear." It was better to set her words lightly, so that the meaning could easily be missed by the people around her.

I don't know, but maybe the reason I got her character wrong was because I'd met Amy's mother only at the end of her life and didn't have the fuller image that Amy had.

***

AMY:

It's always been hard for me to write a character reflective of myself. I've always seen myself not as the principal actor but the lens.

STEWART:

This is one of the things that make Ruth such a challenge. In the beginning of the opera she's undefined, like an empty vessel. The process of the opera is filling that vessel with her family history. She eventually becomes full and strong, connected to her past— like Amy. Ruth is a lot like Amy, except she's not as funny. She has none of Amy's quirks.

AMY:

The details of Ruth being a freelance writer, which I also used for a character in *The Joy Luck Club*, was influenced by my being a free-lance writer, paid to write things for people that didn't know how to say it themselves. The funny thing about LuLing and Ruth is that they're both ghostwriters of a sort. They both make their living by creating words, but they both have a complete inability to be reflective of who they are as people. Later, LuLing tries to get this back, and she also puts it in her daughter's head. In the Hong Kong scene, where Ruth becomes her mother, she sees her own hopes, but also faces her mother's fear, despair, and absolute anger.

***

AMY:

There's a scene in the opera where Precious Auntie threatens LuLing with the dragon bone, which was taken directly from a time when my own mother threatened me with a knife when I was sixteen. I'd never written about this in my fiction, but I did include it in an essay in *The Opposite of Fate*. My mother held the blade to my throat for fifteen or twenty minutes, and during that time, I didn't cry. I didn't make a sound. I felt completely dead inside, until a voice started welling up inside me from the depths of my soul and I started screaming, "I want to live! I want to live!"

STEWART:

We were at Amy's house talking about having Precious Auntie threaten LuLing, and Amy said, "Well, you know, something like that actually happened to me." I hadn't heard any of this before. So after she told us about the voice inside her, I said, "Amy, Ning can be that voice." Amy immediately got very excited about the possibilities. Suddenly we would have a layering of voices that would bypass barriers of time and space, and we could cut right through to the spirit of the book with a primarily musical approach.

AMY:

I realize it can be hard to understand how a mother could do something like that to her own child, but this was something that ran very deep in my mother. She could become so upset with what could go wrong in my life—just like those warnings that we used in the Mink Coat Aria—that she would rather see me dead now than let me ruin my life gradually. That's how strongly she believed in fate. It was her way of saving me, in a strange sense. It has led to many themes of violence in my writing, and questioning what the underlying nature of violence might be.

STEWART:

One of the questions that Zheng had asked me was, "After all that happened, how could Ruth forgive her mother?" I said, "So what do you want, an aria?" To me it makes perfect sense. The real point is that Zheng's role is Ruth in the present *and* LuLing in the past. These aren't separate roles, but rather one long line that runs through the opera.

As we watch Zheng in both present and past, we perceive her as one person experiencing it all, and the knowledge of her mother's past allows her to forgive. At this point in her life she sees her mother fading away, and that marks a profound turning point in a relationship.

AMY:

Also, Ruth has just returned from living through her mother's life in China. It doesn't make LuLing a great parent, but at least Ruth understands that whatever her mother did came from a different history and a sense of protection and love. I was fortunate, in that I had this kind of resolution within myself long before my mother apologized. The process was certainly complete by the time I finished writing *The Joy Luck Club*. By that time, I knew what she was saying, and she knew what I was saying. We'd reached that kind of understanding.

IV.
FINDING A COMMON
LANGUAGE

STEWART:

Most of the time, when I've heard Chinese-born composers using English texts, what they write sounds fake to me. Especially if they try to compose something evoking Chinese opera, the musical gestures sound false and the whole thing takes on an ersatz quality. I could never figure out exactly why until I started working with QianYi. Whenever she'd sing, I'd ask her to break it down so I could see how the words related to the music, even though I had no idea what the words meant. The inherent sound of the words turned out to be extremely crucial to the overall musical effect, which proved to me that the problem using English in Chinese-opera style was not necessarily that English was unsuitable for the music, but rather that the composers lacked a deep, intuitive knowledge of the language's subtleties.

QIAN YI:

Coming to the West turned my whole approach around. In China, they ask for imitation. The highest praise I would get was for how well I could imitate my teacher. Then I came to America, where it's exactly the opposite. In the West, if you're a painter who only imitates Picasso, you're not worth a penny. Here the only way an artist can fit in is to do something different, so I was forced to do everything entirely opposite of the way I was raised. I had to reach inside my heart, become my own model. I went through a couple of years of serious depression until I could figure out what I really want.

STEWART:

The first time I worked with Tian, he had no idea what I wanted him to do, and I realized that our initial obstacle was the English language. When we sat down together with Chang's aria, I soon grew to realize I had to interpret both the spoken language and the musical language for him to understand the musical line and its emotional meaning.

HAO JING TIAN:

The last time I learned a role in a new opera was in Guo Wenjing's *Poet Li Bai*. There, too, I was also playing a Chinese character, but it was a very different experience because that opera was written in Chinese. I was able to step into the character immediately because I felt every single word deeply and intensely. Then I worked with Stewart, which was much more challenging. Stewart can be pushy, with very strong ideas. But he's also very sensitive, which you can hear in his music. Most importantly, though, he's a fabulous coach. He taught me to pronounce English just like him. Part of the problem was that when we first met, I hadn't read Amy's book. But after working with Stewart, I understood exactly what he wants.

NING:

Sometimes working with Stewart I get very irritated. He has spent many hours on his music, so of course he tries his best to persuade us to do it exactly the way he wants. It can be difficult, because English is not my first language. It's particularly difficult to sing because Stewart doesn't always use standard pronunciation, and asks for specific expressions and emotions. We have to be nasty sometimes, and it's up to me to find a way to do this without hurting my voice.

ZHENG:

When we first started working together, Stewart would ask me to sing the same line over and over with slightly different vocal colors. We found colors I didn't even know I had. When Amy saw us work together, I think she was taken aback by the slowness of the process. She asked me, "Doesn't that bug you?" Believe me, it's better to have someone tell you what they want right up front than to show up all prepared for the first day of rehearsal and find out they want something else.

STEWART:

Part of the reason I started working with QianYi was that, despite the challenge, I knew she would be a great teacher, and together we could create something new. It was similar in a way to working with Zhonghua, since both of them would essentially give me sounds, and an entire approach to their art, that I could understand on an intuitive level and translate into my own voice. Later, by working with them in more depth, I could find ways to transfer those things across the length of the whole opera. Sometimes those Chinese elements come into confrontation with my voice. Sometimes my music absorbs them. Sometimes those elements are implied and not actually heard. I'm not sure whether it was because being an outsider I was naturally attuned to everything, but things just popped out at me at every turn. Sometimes they revealed themselves only when I started to compose. When I think back about the experience, the hardest part to write was the restaurant scene in San Francisco. The easiest parts were the scenes in China. It's clear that going to China had a profound effect on *The Bonesetter's Daughter*, and what I've learned in the past few years has profoundly and permanently changed both me and my music.

CHAPTER 5

DESTINY:

ACHIEVING A COLLECTIVE DESTINY

During a recording session for the *Bonesetter* demo, well before the opera was completed, Hao Jiang Tian got his first glimpse of Amy and Stewart's creative process. By then, he was no stranger to new operas or to having characters written especially for him, but Tian's previous roles had come to him the old-fashioned way, with words and music fully formed. After the recording session, Tian discovered from the librettist herself that what she'd heard him sing that afternoon would probably affect his scenes to come.

With its combination of music, singing, acting, visual design, and movement, opera embodies a greater multiplicity of influences than any other art form except film. In the case of the latter—"director's cuts" notwithstanding—the result is a finished document, not an ongoing exploration open to fresh interpretation. Film directors may have editors, but opera composers have conductors and performers embodying their ideas in real time. Stewart often compares Amy's libretto to a screenplay, and the opera composer to a film director, and to a large degree the comparison is apt.

Even by the collaborative standards of opera it's fair to say that *The Bonesetter's Daughter* was more a communal effort than most. Director Chen Shi-Zheng was responsible for several key decisions affecting both the structure and the flow of the piece. Then there were also the performers to consider.

Western opera history is filled with roles tailored to the abilities of specific singers. In the case of *Bonesetter*, however, more than the singers' opinions and vocal ability were involved. For Ning Liang, it was her actual vocal quality and commanding presence; for Zheng Cao, her ability to connect emotionally with her immediate surroundings; and for *kunju* performer Qian Yi, her entire tradition and negotiating its relationship to Western composed music.

Our rational age often has difficulty with words like *fate* and *destiny*. Not so Amy Tan, whose fascination with fate has fueled her fiction and inspired the title of an essay collection. But what better word to describe this opera's very existence? Stewart Wallace, a New York–based composer best known for immortalizing the "Mayor of Castro Street," returning to collaborate with one of the Bay Area's most beloved novelists? David Gockley, the composer's most significant champion on the operatic stage, moving from Houston to the San Francisco Opera at precisely the moment Stewart and Amy could move forward with their project? Or even the composer's original concept—a more traditional operatic model making the younger, more innocent woman a soprano—turning on its head after meeting the singers who would eventually create his roles?

Most of the time, those collaborative influences are defined in musical terms. *The Bonesetter's Daughter*, though, has also been a case of personal synergies affecting the process. Zheng, a former Czech-speaking Varvara in Janacek's *Katya Kabanova* and a cockney-accented Mrs. Lovett in *Sweeney Todd*, has never before played a Chinese character on the operatic stage. Tian and Ning have both played Chinese roles, but never one written by an American-born composer. Qian Yi and Wu Tong have both worked with American composers, but have never been featured in a full-length, through-composed work.

What particularly resonates about these singers is that, having all been born in China and come to the West, their own lives often mirror the themes and situations they portray. Each has admitted to drawing on personal experiences. Zheng confessed that she saw in LuLing's initial dislocation in Hong Kong a vague reflection of her own arrival in America. Ning sees the multicultural, multigenerational dynamic in Amy's American-born Chinese characters being played out in Beijing today. Tian, whose grandparents came from the north, feels a neighborly kinship to LuLing's family, and in a moment of candor expressed a certain affinity for his own character of Chang, whose unselfconscious malevolence taps a well of ill will over which Tian himself—a survivor of the Cultural Revolution—has maintained strict control.

In these and many other regards, the cast and creators of *The Bonesetter's Daughter* all share a creative destiny. They are all like the village where they were born.

1.

THE ACTORS SHAPE THE STORY

HAO JIANG TIAN:

There was one rehearsal right before a two-hour recording session when I worked with Stewart eye to eye, nose to nose. Amy Tan and Sarina Tang also came. They were all sitting behind the glass, but all I could see was Stewart gesturing a lot with his hands. Amy just stepped aside and started writing the whole time. So after it was all over, I asked her, "Are you working on a new book?"

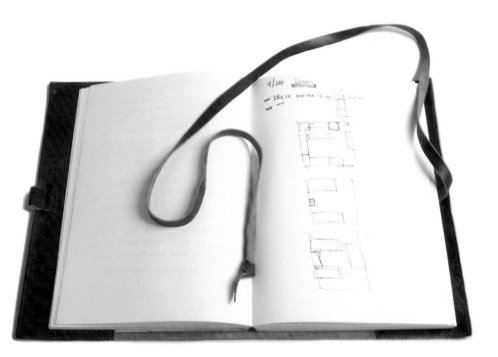

Amy and her leather-bound notebook were inseparable even in Dimen, a Dong village in southeast Guizhou. Drawn to the Dong people's way of life, Amy took extensive notes on their music, their handicrafts, and even the architecture of their houses.

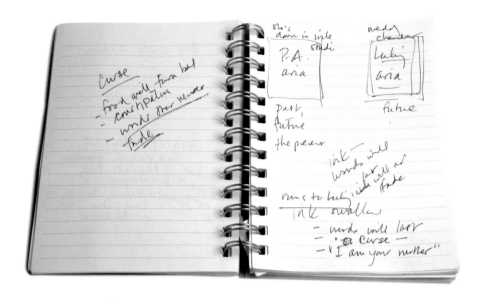

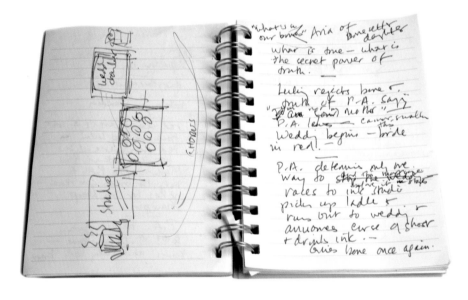

"My notebooks are filled with phrases that can be transformed in some way by using them in different contexts," explains Amy, whose journal entries not only reveal her initial thoughts on Precious Auntie's aria and curse (top) but also sketch out a narrative road map for LuLing's encounter with Precious Auntie over Chang (bottom). Note Amy's visualization of the ink studio. "When I'm in the middle of writing a scene, I have to have a sense of where I am," Amy says.

You:
~~I am a slave~~
Who am I to you?
~~was~~ I was once the
daughter of the
Famous Bonesetter
of Immortal Heart,
now a slave,
~~Not pitiful only in~~
~~Another's eye.~~
low in your eyes.
Was I wrong to save your life
so you could be a slave
by my side?
Who am I ~~to you~~?
~~Not Two slaves~~
Nor a mother to you

Amy's preliminary sketch for Precious Auntie's self-introduction in the Prologue.

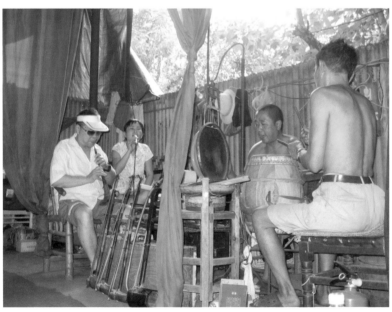

The polyphonic singing styles of the Dong people, which Stewart encountered at a singing class with a master singer (top), heavily influenced the choruses in The Bonesetter's Daughter. *The sounds of Sichuan opera's earthy percussion and piercing* suona *(bottom) made their way into Stewart's opening Dragon Dance.*

Percussionist Li Zhonghua gets his first look at Stewart's score at Sarina Tang's Beijing apartment (top), and Zhonghua makes a demo recording at a Peking Opera recording studio in downtown Beijing (bottom). Stewart says, "Basically, he would show me things from his tradition and I would mess them up."

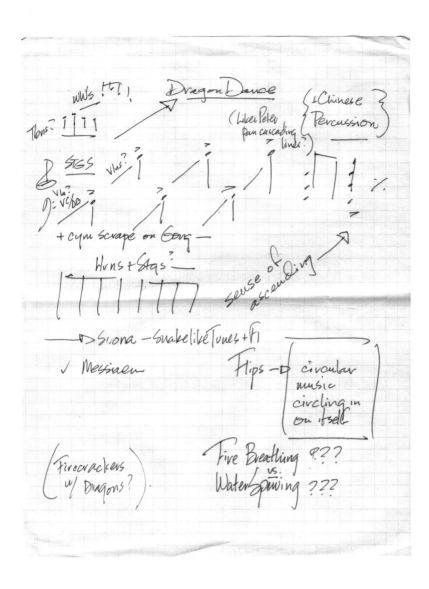

OPERA

Luck foods for New-Years

○ Noodles bar should not be
cut (shorten life)
○ Fish - yu sounds like with
& abundance - head attached
○ sticky rice cakes, sweet
life, rich
○ pomelos - abundance
○ whole chicken - family togetherness
○ clams - symbolize wealth -
resemble good bullion,
○ Lotus seed - male offspring
○ Ging ko net - silver ingots
○ Black moss seaweed -
sounds like exceeding in wealth

The opening scene of the opera in the Fountain Court restaurant at Chinese New
Year traces back to Amy's notes of auspicious foods for the holidays. Amy's "whole
chicken—family togetherness" eventually became the Chef's line, "Happy, Happy,
Happy, Happy Family Chicken. Special for You."

ACT ONE

SCENE ONE

The Fountain Court Chinese Restaurant

San Francisco, February 1997

Firecrackers explode.

A **New Year's Dragon** is led on stage by **Chef** (playing Suona), another Suona and a Snare Drum followed by **Waiters** and a **Marching Band** of 3 Trumpets, 4 Trombones, Tuba, Bass Drum and Crash Cymbals.

The band surrounds a table that reveals a seemingly happy family: **Ruth Young Kamen**, her husband **Art Kamen**, her mother **Luling Young** in a red Chinese jacket, step-daughters **Fia** and **Dory**, and in-laws **Marty** and **Arlene Kamen**.

Precious Auntie, a ghost in clothes from another age and world, stands off to the side, doing a dance of sorts or making enigmatic repetitive gesture. She is beautiful but her mouth is a blackened hole.

Act I opens at the Fountain Court, "partly because it was my mother's favorite restaurant," Amy says, "but also because it was a noisy family place where anything could happen."

"*Amy's writing has a lot of metaphors. The problem when we get to the stage is that there are so many symbols that you have to sort through them all to figure out what the story is about visually. I usually like to focus on the simplest iconic elements in a way that turns cliché into myth.*"

—CHEN SHI-ZHENG, DIRECTOR

Shi-Zheng unveils The Bonesetter's Daughter *set design by Walter Spangler, explaining to the San Francisco Opera staff how the set models fit together.*

Two scenes of a restaurant: The initial visual of the Fountain Court, created immediately following the Bonesetter *creative team's preliminary meeting, with multimedia projections indicating a restaurant fish tank (top), and a three-dimensional model suggesting how the cast and acrobatic waiters would fill the scene (bottom).*

"I didn't want to be involved in this project. Amy's book was about China, and I didn't want to remember China. But then I heard Stewart's music, and I couldn't believe how beautiful it was. Later, director Chen Shi-Zheng explained, 'Amy's book is the old China. Stewart's music is today.' So that inspired me to have the clothes tell a story. Yes, it's China, but it's a different China than you think."

—HAN FENG, COSTUME DESIGNER

TOP *Shi-Zheng introduces Han Feng's designs to the San Francisco Opera staff.*

ABOVE *The three women of the family—Ruth (Zheng Cao), LuLing (Ning Liang), and Precious Auntie (QianYi)—emerge from the San Francisco fog in the Prologue.*

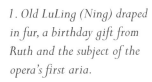

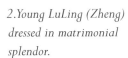

1

2

3

4

5

6

1. Old LuLing (Ning) draped in fur, a birthday gift from Ruth and the subject of the opera's first aria.

2. Young LuLing (Zheng) dressed in matrimonial splendor.

3. Chang (Hao Jiang Tian) dressed in matrimonial splendor.

4. Wu Tong as the Restaurant Owner in the opening scene.

5. Wu Tong as the Taoist Priest dressed to lead Ruth into the past.

6. Wu Tong as the Taoist Priest dressed to preside over the wedding of Chang and Young LuLing.

Han Feng's preliminary dress design for the beginning of Act II. Now a ghost, Precious Auntie is suspended above the stage dressed in a tattered flowing gown still singed from the fire at the end of Act I.

Precious Auntie returns at the end of Act II in this preliminary, ghostly white Han Feng design, preparing to guide her dying daughter LuLing through the fog to another world.

TRANSITION

BETWEEN WORLDS

The shadow bends down and caresses Ruth's other cheek. The music does not
begin until that touch and should feel looser and more improvisatory throughout.

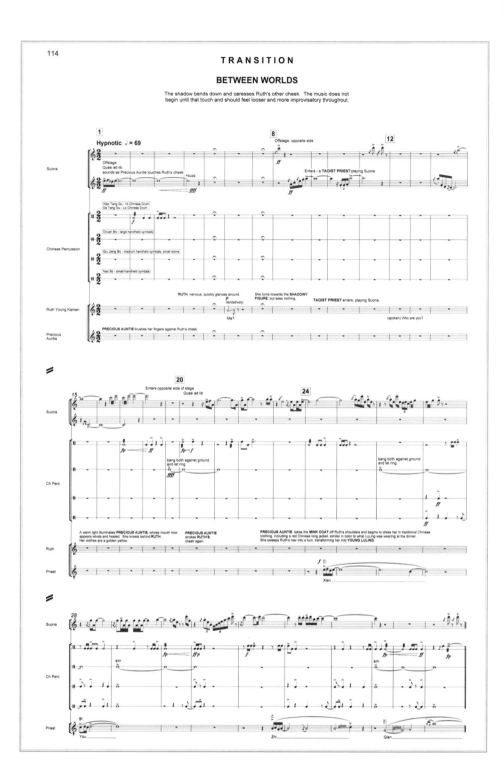

The acrobats who waited tables in Scene 1 return as floating bodies to lead
Ruth into the past in the "Transition: Between Worlds."

She said, "No, I'm adding new things for you." I got a little worried. My guess was that, since my character was pretty bad already, he was going to get a lot worse.

AMY TAN:

That was the first time I'd really heard the way the music and the words fit together with such high-level singing. I was blown away by Tian's voice. It was beautiful and exciting, and it really enlarged what I could see in the libretto. What made me start writing, though, was the way Stewart was directing. He was adamant that Tian enunciate certain things, and extend the ends of certain words. I was already thinking of what I could do to put in more sibilants—those hissy, buzzy sounds that Stewart likes a lot.

STEWART WALLACE:

Tian wasn't kidding when he said we were nose to nose. When we rehearsed his aria the first time, I realized he had learned it entirely wrong. It was the language—not the pronunciation but the colorations and phrasing, and even some of the meanings—that he didn't understand at all.

TIAN:

English is, of course, not my native language. With Amy's words, I feel that I need a lot of time to swallow and digest them. I wasn't worried about the diction and pronunciation because I have experience in so many languages. But I needed to feel them. Otherwise they sound artificial. They have to be in your blood. The problem with Amy's story is that I recognized all the words, but after a while I realized they did not always mean what I thought they did. Stewart had to tell me that when I was singing about "Chang's old wood," I was really talking about my dick.

AMY:

It was watching the rehearsal process that was the most fun, and until someone said something about the way Stewart works, it never had occurred to me that there was anything special about it. Now I'll ask singers, "Has any other composer directed you with this kind of attention to color and nuance?" They'll say, "No, not at all."

STEWART:

I have to work like that. For me, it's part of the language of the music, and if the singers don't understand that, their performance will always sound bad to me. I have to rehearse like that or I'll just be miserable.

***

AMY:

Once we heard Ning, there was no question that we really had to find excuses to use her more. Fortunately we had also been looking at new ways to tell the story that would let us bring Ning back in the picture and also make dramatic sense.

STEWART:

Ning really insinuated herself as Old LuLing in the scenes in China, which was very far from our original plans. Part of it came out of story decisions we had made independent of hearing Ning, but it was also largely the strength of Ning's personality, and realizing that she was the kind of person who would find her way to the past even though she wasn't supposed to be there. Amy and I had talked about the voice that wells up in Young LuLing when Precious Auntie has the knife to her throat, so I said to Amy, "We've been thinking of ways to bring Old LuLing back into the scene. She's that voice." It's funny, because both Ning the singer and LuLing the character share this trait of not liking to be ignored. I think the two of them conspired to make sure that they would be in this scene.

***

AMY:

One year, a friend was murdered on my birthday, and I was the one who had to identify the body. It was horrible. For several years after this, I lost my voice on my birthday, which is a trait I gave Ruth in the novel, a psychological response to something unspeakable. In my case, I still have that horrible image every year. You know all those movies you see with bloody corpses? The thing they can't show you is what the room smells like. Behind everyone there's a trauma that reverberates in their life, and I think all artists have things like this that permeate our work.

STEWART:

You know the story of what happened with Shi-Zheng during the Cultural Revolution? We were down at the Spoleto Festival when I asked him what happened to his family. He told me that his mother was shot by a stray bullet right in front of him when he was a child. I was astounded when I heard that story. Even more astounding was that we were around the *Peony Pavilion* technical crew and I saw all their jaws drop. Shi-Zheng had been working with them for years and they had never known.

AMY:

But did you hear about the image that he saw? It wasn't only that his mother was shot, but the bullet whizzed over his head and entered her from the side. He doesn't quite know what happened. They put her on the back of the truck bed and lay a sheet over her. And from that bullet hole there's a small red dot that keeps getting bigger until the whole sheet is completely red. Where do you think that image went? It comes through in all his work.

CHEN SHI-ZHENG:

What has haunted me about Amy's story is that it's about the past. Those of us who lived through the Cultural Revolution have tried to forget our past. The past is always there, so big that you can't compress it. But Amy's approach to memory is to go back and dig it out, like archaeology. She goes back and opens the wounds because they will always haunt you until you come to terms with them. It starts out as Amy's story, but it becomes the story of everyone who's ever had to carry their past with them.

11.

FEELING THE CHARACTERS

TIAN:

I feel that I am at an age in my career that if I don't do something different, some part of me will simply die artistically. Of the new operas I've done, *The First Emperor* was set two thousand years ago, and *Poet Li Bai* was set twelve hundred years ago. Now, *The Bonesetter's Daughter* is set seventy years ago. At this rate, someone will soon be writing something for me set in today's time. But I must say, of the fifty or so operas I've done, this one is completely different. I like the music very much because it is very American. I don't know how to describe it, but the melody, the tempo, the energy are all American—and particularly very New York. I think if Stewart lived in Jackson Hole, Wyoming, *Bonesetter's Daughter* would be a completely different show.

NING LIANG:

There is a lot of truth in the way Amy captures the three generations. She dramatizes, of course, but she also understands how in the old generation—my parents' generation—the people who left and the people who stayed in China had entirely different lives. Just like me now with my friends who never left in twenty years, we have entirely different living styles. I like to surround myself with cultured things in my home, but when I visit friends in Beijing, especially the rich friends, I feel like I'm in a five-star hotel. There is no character, no heart there. We may both live in China, but we are having entirely different experiences.

TIAN:

As I read the book—the Chinese translation—I could actually feel the characters. There are usually similarities with Chinese families, but my mother's family was also from Shanxi province. And just like the family in the story, hers was a big, important family that after one generation started going down. Also, my grandfather used to work in Beijing at an antique store in the 1920s, which is about the same period as the story. They could have been LuLing's neighbors.

ZHENG CAO:

The fact that my character is Chinese, or Chinese American, doesn't have any bearing on my preparation. Whether I'm playing a Chinese, Russian, or Czech person, I will always throw myself into a role. But maybe because she's Chinese I can use my own background, instead of relying so much on research or on the help of coaches. This is a role where I can benefit from my own internal conflicts, like in the second act, when Young LuLing is walking around the Hong Kong harbor, saying, "I'm no one, I have nowhere to go to." I can definitely remember my own desperation when I first came to the United States.

NING:

This role has become very natural for me because on a certain level I play myself—well, I shouldn't say that, because I play an old lady. But there are parts of it that I can really relate to. It's tempting to say, "I'm Chinese, so I can play Chinese." It's much more than that. It has to be part of you, and you have to know yourself. You have to be able to study yourself in a mirror, which in opera can be more difficult than playing someone from another time and place.

SHI-ZHENG:

Amy's perspective is not the perspective of someone who was born in China, but you can see very clearly how she's navigated her way through the country, just as anyone who comes out or in has to find their own way. What I find so interesting about Amy is that she has taken exactly the opposite of my own path, having come out of China and gone to the West. This project exists right at the juncture where we meet. It's hard to say about *Bonesetter's Daughter* which part is Chinese and which part is Western. It never falls into a formula, because the way the story is written there's no formula to fall into. We take San Francisco out of San Francisco, and China out of China, and create a world where both can exist on equal terms.

QIAN YI:

What Amy offers isn't only American, or Chinese. For a daughter to hear the stories from her mother and grandmother is very universal. What Stewart offers is entirely different. Most Chinese people think of Western opera as very high art. Lincoln Center and Carnegie Hall are palaces where people wear tuxedos. Stewart's composition is not at all like that. Even when he listens to Chinese music, he goes for Sichuan opera—very raw music, very *chaanng, chaaang, chaaang, tika-tika-tika*—not refined art like the *kunju* I perform. But in both Western and Chinese music, Stewart has this ability to find a place where raw and refined music can exist together.

LI ZHONGHUA:

This show to me represents a complete change in thought process. When I do my usual traditional performances, I don't think there will be much difference. But in terms of thinking creatively, in using my own tradition of Peking Opera to absorb other traditions and see what we all can come up with together, this is a wonderful beginning.

111.

IT'S ALL ABOUT THE STORY

MICHAEL KORIE:

I know firsthand how wonderful Stewart is as a collaborator. The best stage composers are also librettists, in a matter of speaking.

They have a firm grasp on how the information and drama should come out through the music. They can pace themselves. They know the importance of transitions and scene breaks. Some composers, brilliant as they may be, lack that conception. Take Prokofiev's *War and Peace*. Musically, it's a wonderful opera, but dramatically it's a total cheat because the librettist basically says, "We're only going to do a couple of scenes—if you want the story you'll have to read the book." At that point, it just becomes a purely intellectual experience in comparing source material. What Stewart and Amy are doing is entirely different. It's an opera where the viewer doesn't necessarily have to be initiated beforehand, and the focus is equally on the story and the way the music tells it.

Shi-Zheng:

This is not like most operas, where each of the creators works entirely in his or her own sphere. And that process has also shaped the piece. So much of opera is focused on the performance. Here, it's all about the story, and having such a close collaboration has helped Amy and Stewart keep any one element from taking too much away from the story.

David Gockley:

The opera obviously owes a lot to Stewart's research in China, not only in his discovery of the instruments and musical sounds, but also in its incorporation of ceremonial things like funerals and weddings. Ceremony usually works well in opera. You've got religious ceremonies in *Aida*, for example, and Wagner latched on to the song contest, which was a very big thing in the Middle Ages. Even *Harvey Milk* had the Gay Pride Parade, complete with baton twirlers in drag and "Dykes on Bikes." My advice would always be, if you've got a ceremony, put it in. I'm not sure that Stewart would've been so aware of China's ceremonial aspect if he hadn't made those trips. They were all crucial in creating the opera's musical shape and substance.

TIAN:

As far as the story is concerned, I think the fact that the music rep-
resenting China comes from a totally different perspective is a
good thing. American people don't really know much about China.
Maybe they know the Cultural Revolution and perhaps something
about Mao. But ask what happened in the Pacific region during
World War II, and they know nothing except Pearl Harbor. That's
why this opera is important—it will help people learn something
about a certain period in China through a composer's language
they can understand.

NING:

You know, the opera opens with a *suona*—two *suonas*—and I tell you,
I never liked that instrument. It hurts my ears like a loud soprano.
But that opening! It is very brave, and extremely Chinese. Not even
[composer] Tan Dun has done something so extreme.

DAVID:

I first heard about the possibility of this opera when I was still general director of the Houston Grand Opera, but I must say I was
more interested in the piece once I got to San Francisco. The whole
story of the opera is essentially about moving to this city, specifi-
cally the Chinese population. But underneath those details, the
story is relevant to anyone who's ever moved to America and
become set apart from their homeland, and their heritage.

SHI-ZHENG:

The question will come up at some point: is this a Chinese opera or
a Western opera? I've already gotten complaints from the Chinese
side that in shows like *Monkey* I'm watering down Chinese culture
and catering it to the West, and I can already hear what some people
in the other camp might say about Amy and Stewart—that they're
trying to cater to China. It's easy for either side to pick out a few
examples of our work and say that. But the situation is rarely that
simple. Art is human. Its only reason for existence is to make sense

of human attributes. What I find most striking about *The Bonesetter's Daughter* is that its comedy and tragedy weigh the same, which is a trait that is not exclusive to either China or the West. No matter what people say, ultimately, as an artist, I first have to please myself, just as Amy and Stewart have to please themselves.

QIAN YI:

Most of the shows I've done since *Peony Pavilion* have been criticized by the purists. They think that whenever you perform Chinese opera to Westerners automatically you dilute the culture. But look at our own tradition. A fundamental part of Chinese opera is that you have to please the audience. If the audience doesn't get the references, then you present them in a way that they will. Connecting with audiences is a crucial part of our artistic culture because without that we have nothing.

LI ZHONGHUA:

Most of the time, when Chinese opera uses Western-style instrumentation, the instruments stick out. A Western orchestra makes a very strange accompaniment to that performance style. Getting the balance is always tricky. You have to tilt toward the Western side, I think, because the tolerance for Western culture in China is much higher than Western audiences for Chinese opera. But this is a fresh collaboration. This time I think we've made a true mingling of Eastern and Western culture.

IV.

AN ACCIDENTAL CONCEPT

STEWART:

One of the things that makes the music fully in character with Amy's books is that our three principal singers are all essentially mezzo-sopranos and, despite the differences in their vocal style and tone color, all are essentially part of each other—kind of like Don Giovanni and Leporello, but in triplicate. I wish we could both claim this had been our grand scheme from the beginning, but that happened in part because we found Zheng and I no longer felt we needed a soprano. One of the joys of doing this show was that we kept learning along the way, and we kept meeting amazing people who kept affecting the choices we made.

AMY:

My only concern about casting was that the performers could emote. One of my pet peeves about opera has always been when people just stand there singing to the audience without any connection to the other characters on stage. With *Bonesetter* in particular, the story has so much to do with emotion *among* the characters that an emotive approach was essential. When I saw Zheng perform in *Madame Butterfly*, she had the strongest emotive quality in the cast. She also had to have both strength and naïveté, which was a duality inherent in the character so she could be transformed later.

STEWART:

You also wanted them to be good-looking, I remember. Particularly the men. You said they had to be sexy.

AMY:

That was definitely true for Art. Whenever anyone was suggested who wasn't particularly handsome, I'd say no. I'd have to believe that the person would be attractive to Zheng. And Zheng liked that idea, too, I should add. But there has to be a certain chemistry between Art and Ruth. You need to believe that something is at stake here. What I've hated most about many of the productions of *Madame Butterfly* I've seen is that you really don't care when Pinkerton goes off. It's usually good riddance. He usually doesn't have a body, and nothing about him conveys any trace of sexuality. It makes me want to scream, "You're killing yourself for *him*?"

* * *

STEWART:

I've been wondering, Amy, when you hear your words set to music, do you feel that the emotions get heightened?

AMY:

I think I'll need to hear the opera all the way through before I can answer that. It's like reading only part of a short story. A story deserves to be read from the beginning to end in one breath, and an opera is very similar. Once I see the whole thing from start to finish, that will define the emotional experience to me.

STEWART:

But even when you hear fragments of the piece, you respond emotionally.

AMY:

Well, yes, I've been very moved emotionally. I was even cheerful, I should probably add. I was struck by how beautiful it sounds, and could feel each emotional point as it was happening. But being in the moment isn't everything. There's a shape, a build-up, an arc of the story that has to mount. It's like orgasm, you can't just jump to the high points. You have to have the build-up—otherwise it doesn't make sense.

STEWART:

What about hearing your words in the mouths of other people? When Zheng or Ning sings your text, does it hit you in the way you'd expect, or is it surprising?

AMY:

It's interesting that we've been talking so much about music and text. I never think in terms of text. I think of writing in terms of words and voice, and to me the voice is the most important thing in anything I write. That's probably the number-one question for writers: What's your voice? The voice is not fiction. The voice is what the person knows and believes, what they see, what they think about the world, the nature of their character, and how they've been shaped by history. All of this goes into the voice. It's not the voice that's on the page, but the voice is the source of every word. Whenever I start to write, I have to know the voice before the words will come. So when I hear an actual, physical voice singing my words, that becomes the personification of my internal voice. The wonderful thing about opera is that the singers' voices are so refined, so nuanced, so full of resonance. The story in any opera has to have emotional resonance, and an opera singer's voice has to have that physical quality.

STEWART:

That sounds like something you've been thinking about for a while now. The first thing I think about when I start an opera is, "What's the sound world, the universe of the piece?" Each opera is its own world, and while it's all grounded in the voice of the composer, each one has its own unique qualities and quirks. But what I originally meant was, what did you think the first time you heard your words sung?

AMY:

The first time I heard them sung I was overcome with self-consciousness. I kept thinking, I should have done better. I can't believe they're *singing* this. I was fine with it on the page, but I'm embarrassed now that it's out there in the ether. The story is a very close emotional experience to me. It's true to my own life. And when things happen in the opera that are different from what really happened, I have to ask myself, is it different because it should be different for the sake of the story, or different because the emotion doesn't seem to be right? This doesn't mean you have to have lived my life to enjoy the opera. Sarina said that the first time she heard the music played through, she had to leave because she was so emotionally overwrought. It reminded her of her own relationship with her mother, except that they never had the same resolution before her mother died. Everyone has a different reaction, which is as it should be. Why does *Madame Butterfly* resonate so much with so many people? That's probably the one opera that gets people to love the art more than any other, but not every woman kills herself and sends her baby away.

'V.

'FINDING TRUTH IN 'PAST AND 'PRESENT

STEWART:

I've been thinking about the way we use Precious Auntie to help take the story back physically into a different world, and I feel a certain echo from *The Hundred Secret Senses*, showing the membrane between past and present being rather fluid. It shows that the way you approached this project was not just as this particular story, but as a connection to all of your stories. It was not literally re-creating the book but about preserving its spiritual and emotional truth while freely borrowing from your other work. In a way, it's the difference between writing your first piece and your sixth. That first contains all your ambitions, goals, and desires. As you go on, all of your pieces become a part of each other because they share the same DNA. If we'd decided to do this years ago, say, when you'd just written *The Joy Luck Club* and I'd written *Where's Dick?*, it would've been a completely different experience.

AMY:

I know I repeat myself a lot in my books, and sometimes I think it's a flaw. But when I look back and find a recurrent theme or characteristic, I realize it's also integral to that particular story. For example, in every single book someone is making a journey to China that propels the story forward. It might be a physical journey, or it might be someone reading a letter, but every book starts in the present, goes into the past, and comes back again to the present changed. It's a typical method of transformation—just think of *The Wizard of Oz*—but I'd always done this even before I knew it was an accepted pattern, partly because I really did travel to China. This was a literary approach that resonated particularly well with me because that's how it happened in real life. When I start to write, I feel like I become my mother, or whoever the character is. I have to become that character.

STEWART:

That's exactly what I have to do when I compose: perform the characters or channel them in some way that I have to find in music. The composer is like the director in a film because you dictate the tone and the rhythm of the way things will happen in time and space. And like a director, I have to get possessed with what I know to be the character. Because of the medium, it's a couple of steps removed, but the idea is the same.

AMY:

Feeling the emotions is a large part of it. But when I'm in the middle of writing a scene, I have a sense of looking to the left and right, of seeing what I'm wearing. I have to know what the temperature is. And I can change the scene on command, which is something I've learned from my dreams. If I don't like a particular dream I'm having, I can change it just by looking down at my shoes. When I look up, the perspective will be entirely changed.

STEWART:

That sounds like *The Wizard of Oz* again, with the ruby slippers.

AMY:

I don't actually click my heels, but to change the perspective all I have to do is look down. Once I learned to control my dreams that way, I realized that it was a great metaphor for life, as well as fiction.

***

STEWART:

Amy and I didn't have many fights, but she was concerned about Precious Auntie cleaning the blood from Chang's dick off of the dragon bone before she gives it back to Young LuLing. I kept saying, "I know you're a good Chinese girl who's concerned about hygiene, but we really don't have time to worry about the dick blood."

AMY:

It wasn't a cleanliness thing—it was an emotional thing. But I was really concerned for a while about your and Shi-Zheng's obsession with destruction. For the longest time, my draft contained the two scenarios at the end of Act I:

> BOYS' VERSION: *Blood pours out and wipes out everything, stage is ruined, patrons flee for their lives covered in colored water that stains very expensive velvet seats and designer clothes. Audience becomes chorus, "Lawsuit! Lawsuit!" Stewart and Shi-Zheng's long-cherished wish fulfilled. Amy nervous, but relieved she already signed liability waiver.*

> AMY'S VERSION: *More symbolic imagery of destruction, simple but more powerful than expensive and dangerous boys' version. Viewers moved to tears, but not angry and ready to kill opera staff.*

Sometimes I'm not really sure I understand opera.

***

AMY:

We've talked about your playing in a band, Stewart, but you know I'm in a band, too [the Rock-Bottom Remainders, with fellow writers Stephen King and Dave Barry, among others]. And the thing I've learned most about being in a band is that it's not about the songs. It's not even about your singing. It's about performance. What you do every night is communicate with your audience. I used to hate giving speeches, saying the same thing over and over like a little rat on a treadmill. But you realize after a while that performance is its own art. You may be using the same material over and over, but the audience is different, and you have to find a new way to connect with them every night. That was key to my writing a libretto. Yes, you have to provide structure and leave room for music, but right from the start with this opera I was always thinking purely from my gut, trying to focus on those key emotional points. I'm not sure at the beginning I could've done that with any other opera, but this story I knew very well. I knew what would be true.

THE
BONESETTER'S
DAUGHTER

LIBRETTO BY AMY TAN
BASED ON HER NOVEL

MUSIC BY STEWART WALLACE

ACT **1**

PROLOGUE ≠
DRAGON DANCE

A TIMELESS VOID

A loud, reedy, braying call. An answering call comes from across the void. Two Dragons appear: a water dragon and a fire dragon. The dragons levitate and cross, making smoke from water and fire. Out of the fog appear the three women of the family: Ruth, a modern-day American woman; LuLing, an older woman of another generation; and Precious Auntie, a ghost from another world, holding a Dragon Bone.

PRECIOUS AUNTIE, LuLING, RUTH
  These are the things.
  These are the things I know.
  These are the things I know are true.

RUTH
  My name is Ruth Young Kamen.
  I live in San Francisco, in the fog.
  When I was a child, my mother told me
  the fog comes from the nostrils of two giant dragons.

LuLING
  These are the things . . .

RUTH
  She is a fire dragon.
  I am a water dragon.
  We were both born in dragon years.

LuLING
  We are the same
  for different reasons.

RUTH
>Together

LuLING, RUTH
>We Make Fog.

PRECIOUS AUNTIE, LuLING, RUTH
>These are the things
>I know.
>Pain and regret and sorrow.
>These are the things
>I know.
>Desire and hope and love.
>These things I have known
>but not enough, not long enough.
>If only I could remember them all.

LuLING
>My name is LuLing Liu.
>That's the American way.
>In the past it was Liu LuLing,
>the Chinese way,
>backwards from what it is now.

RUTH
>The American way.

PRECIOUS AUNTIE
>These are the things . . .

LuLING
>I was born in China
>in the Village of Immortal Heart.
>Liu LuLing.
>When I say it that way,
>I feel myself again.
>I know what is true.

PRECIOUS AUNTIE, LuLING, RUTH
>These are the things.
>These are the things I know.
>These are the things I know are true.

PRECIOUS AUNTIE
>My name is Precious Auntie.
>That's what everybody called me.
>LuLing called me Precious Auntie, too.
>I live in Immortal Heart, at the Mouth of the Mountain,
>a Mouth that swallows up bones and spits them out!
>My father was the Bonesetter of Immortal Heart,
>And I am the Bonesetter's Daughter.
>I am a ghost now.
>I live in memory.
>A ghost does not live only in the past.
>You see me, don't you?
>Don't you?
>LuLing does not see me.
>Ruth does not see me—yet.

PRECIOUS AUNTIE, LuLING, RUTH
>I am the past.
>I am the present.
>I am the future.

PRECIOUS AUNTIE
>I am like the village where I was born.
>Immortal Heart.
>Immortal Heart.
>Immortal . . .

PRECIOUS AUNTIE, LuLING, RUTH
>Heart.

SCENE 1

FOUNTAIN COURT CHINESE RESTAURANT,

SAN FRANCISCO, FEBRUARY 1997

Explosive firecrackers. A suona *calls. Drums and cymbals sound. The Dragon on the screen transforms and becomes a New Year's Dragon and comes out, along with a marching band playing New Year's Chinese music that evolves into circus music.*

The happy family watches: The girls stand in front of Marty and Arlene, who put their arms around them. Art inserts himself between Ruth and LuLing and puts his arm around Ruth. LuLing stands alone looking at Ruth. Precious Auntie, a ghost in clothes from another age and world, stands off to the side. She is beautiful but her mouth is a blackened hole.

The Dragon Dance becomes more frenzied and impressive . . . and then transforms into waiters in the restaurant who quickly place food on the lazy Susan through elaborate acrobatic moves.

CHEF
Happy, Happy, Happy, Happy
Happy Family Chicken.
(gives the lazy Susan a spin)
Special for you.

MARTY
Is he Jewish?

RUTH
Lucky foods, for Chinese New Year.

CHEF
Two families,
the Youngs,
the Kamens,
happy,
harmonious families,
connected by good Chinese food.

MARTY
I love . . .

ALL
Chinese Food.

DORY
The head.

ARLENE
The feet.

MARTY
And the tail.

FIA
(to Arlene)
I feel sick.

MARTY
Sick?
Artie?
Arlene!

CHEF
No problem, no problem.
You don't like, I chop it off.

ART
(breaks away from Ruth to inspect the chicken)
Ruthie, honey, I told you,
No meat that looks like what it is.

RUTH
I'm sorry.

LULING
Why you sorry?
Not eat such good things, they be sorry.
(to Arlene) Eat some crab.
Crab so good.

ARLENE

> LuLing-dear, it's not a Jewish thing,
> I like shellfish, it doesn't like me.

ART

> Mom?

LuLING

> So many things, they not like you.

RUTH

> Ma?

ARLENE

> It gives me hives.
> Then I can't breathe,
> my throat slams shut,
> bye-bye, it's a coffin for me
> *(she snaps her fingers)*—just like that. *(gongs of death)*

RUTH

> I'm sorry.

ARLENE

> Don't be. I'm not dead yet.

LuLING

> Don't say dead.

MARTY

> You just said it.

LuLING

> What I say?

MARTY, ARLENE, FIA, DORY

> Dead!

LuLING

> Ai-ya!

DORY
> Can't we have something that's never been dead?

LuLING
> You say dead, somebody die.

RUTH
> (*to Fia and Dory, pointing to another dish*)
> Just try.

FIA AND DORY
> I won't.

RUTH
> Just taste.

FIA AND DORY
> You can't make me.
> You're not my mother!

> *Ruth stands straight, stunned. LuLing turns to look at Ruth and also looks stricken. Precious Auntie looks at LuLing.*

LuLING
> Such words.

PRECIOUS AUNTIE
> (*overlapping LuLing*)
> Such words.

LuLING
> So cruel.

PRECIOUS AUNTIE
> They stain.

LuLING
> Such cruel words.

PRECIOUS AUNTIE
> They burn.

LuLing
>They kill.

Precious Auntie and LuLing
>I remember . . .

Marty
>*(congenially to Ruth)*
>Ruthie, sweetheart, don't take it personal.
>Artie's wife never makes 'em eat a thing.

LuLing
>Lootie, she Artie's wife.

Marty
>*(pats LuLing's arm)*
>You know what I mean.

LuLing
>I *know* you mean.

Ruth
>Ma?

Art
>It's okay, girls.
>*(to Ruth)* Noodles?
>With butter?

Ruth
>*(shoots Art a look of chagrin, of betrayal)*
>Doesn't matter.

>*Chef motions to the Waiter. Marching band enters followed by waiters with a birthday cake ablaze with candles burning like torches.*

Chef
>Happy, Happy, Happy, Happy,
>Happy Birthday.

>*LuLing looks as if she will break into tears.*

RUTH
> *(reaches under table and brings out a red box)*
> Happy birthday.
> What you wanted, Ma.

LuLing
> *(opens box and pulls out mink coat, her expression and true emotions playing against what she says in protest)*
> Oh, for me?
> I never want it.
> I don't need it.
> Why you buy me mink coat?

RUTH
> *(tenderly)*
> Touch.

LuLing
> *(murmuring happily)*
> Too much.

ARLENE
> Mink? In this day and age?

ART
> I tried to tell her . . .

DORY and FIA
> Dead animals, yuck!

LuLing
> Don't say . . .

ARLENE
> I wouldn't be caught dead in it!

LuLing
> Ai-ya! Don't say dead.

ARLENE
> Ruthie honey, *really*!

As Ruth sings, LuLing nods, happy to hear Ruth's acknowledgment of her.

RUTH
    She wanted the mink, I think.
    She hinted a lot, but *not*
    To keep her warm,
    Or let her show off.
    But to show I care,
    for all she cared.
    Her worries, endless worries.
    Her advice:

    "Stand straight, no crooked,
    be polite, no talking back.
    Be smart, number one, don't have fun.
    Be humble,
    and don't mumble 'What?'
    when I call your name,
    when I say, come home, you come.
    No running into street
    Or you get squashed flat
    like a sand dab,
    Both eyes stuck
    ai-ya!
    on one side of your head."

    She told me this when I was five.
    And when I was older, I told her,
    I want to go to the dance,
    I wanna wear this dress.
    She said:

    "Why so fancy?
    You want to kiss boys?
    What if you like too much,
    And you can't stop?
    You lose
    your mind,
    that fancy dress,

your panties next.
Then baby come
And cry out: shame you, you bad.
Then you afraid I mad,
So you throw that baby
in garbage can.
Then police,
they coming,
throw you in jail,
no bail.
Your life already over.
Why not kill yourself right now?
So I can't watch
With a knife in my heart,
How you ruin your life."

She told me this
when I was twelve.
Look at me now.
No babies, no jail,
no broken heart.
That's why I bought the mink.

LuLing lightly puts her hand on Ruth's face and caresses her cheek, which embarrasses Ruth.

LuLing
    Such a good daughter!

Ruth
    To prove I was grateful,
    not guilty.

Marty
    I couldna said it better myself!

Arlene
    That's what a ghostwriter does, Marty.
    They talk, she types.

LuLing

> Lootie, you write for ghosts?

Ruth

> Co-writer, Ma, not ghostwriter.

Precious Auntie

> Write for me.
> Speak for me.
> Remember my hopes.
> Forever and ever.
> So I can tell LuLing. . . .

Precious Auntie lightly caresses LuLing's cheek, the same brushing gesture as when Ruth and LuLing brushed fingertips along the mink.

LuLing

> *(glances about, excited)*
> Lootie, you hear ghost?
> you feel her, too?
> Do you?
> Lootie, Quick, write down her ghost words.
> I already waiting so long.

Others look uneasy, wondering if perhaps LuLing is not joking but delusional.

Art

> *(bringing the conversation back to firm reality)*
> Ruth works with very important people.
> Famous, rich, like her client now.
> One of those lawyers from the O.J. trial,
> I forget which one.
> He's writing a book . . . with Ruth . . .
> And Ruth's gotta make it
> fresh,
> unpredictable,
> even though we know O.J. gets off.

Ruth

> Not guilty.

LuLing

> Lootie, I help you write.
> I know this story.

Ruth

> *(a little laugh)*
> Ma, I don't need help.

LuLing

> A daughter always need her mother help.
> I see things you don't.

As LuLing describes the events, she jumps and gestures as if the scene is happening right in front of her.

> That O.J. man go hide in bush.
> Waiting for his wife.
> I hiding there, too.
> Waiting, waiting, both of us waiting.
> I seen them coming.
> His pretty wife, laughing at her friend.
> She get out key, she open door.
> Then O.J. jump out, wah!
> He grab that friend,
> put knife on neck,
> and pull acrosssssss–*szzzt!*
> You don't wanna see.

Fia and Dory make faces and Arlene gestures to Art that this is inappropriate.

> Then oh, so awful,
> So much blood,
> pouring out on the ground.
> And O.J. wife, she scream so scared,
> No, no, don't take my life.
> That O.J. man he use that knife,
> Still dripping blood,
> And pull acrosssssss–*szzzt!*

I told that girl:
If you my daughter
(slowly turns from looking at imaginary corpse to Ruth)
I warn you this,
Open your eyes,
watch your heart,
watch out your husband.
Save your life.

There she lie on ground
Eyes still open,
Seeing nothing now.
Her empty heart.

RUTH
(spoken)
Ma, you're confused . . .
(afraid to voice what she suspects)
Maybe your memory isn't working right.

Everyone nods.

LuLing
Nothing wrong my memory!
Trouble is cannot forget.
Cannot forget my mother
Die so young
Left me alone so I made bad mistakes.
Cannot forget your daddy
Die so young
Left me to raise you lonely
All alone.
You so young, you so shamed of me.
Cannot forget
What you don't see
How you forgetting yourself.

RUTH

> *(spoken)*
> Come on, Ma. It's your birthday.
> Let it go or it'll drive you crazy.

LuLing

> *(false calmness, the eye of the storm)*
> Okay, I crazy.
> Why you should believe?
> Don't listen your mother.
> *(mounting danger, voice rising)*
> Maybe you wish I never your mother.
> You said those words.

RUTH

> *(sensing what is about to follow)*
> Ma, please.
> I was just a kid then!

LuLing

> Maybe you wish I dead.
> You said those words.

RUTH

> I didn't mean it.
> I was only twelve.

LuLing

> *(explosion)*
> Maybe I kill myself right now!
> Then you be happy, happy, happy!
> Then everybody happy!

LuLing flings down the mink coat and turns to leave. Everyone rolls eyes and shakes heads in disgust, suggesting LuLing is histrionic, making a big scene for nothing.

RUTH

> *(to others)*
> Stop her!
> She's tried before!

Ruth runs and grabs her sleeve, and as LuLing violently pulls away, she loses her balance and falls.

RUTH

MA!

Everyone, including the wait staff, freezes and stares. Only Ruth rushes over and kneels down to assess her mother, who is moaning.

LuLING

Ai-ya, now I die for sure.

RUTH

Don't say that word.

LuLing grimaces and groans in pain. Ruth rocks her like a baby, crying. While she sings, there is commotion in the background.

Restaurant Owner motions waiters to summon help. Soon emergency medical technicians arrive with a stretcher. Arlene and Marty gesture for the girls to leave. Art nods at their decision, and they exit.

RUTH

You'll be fine, Ma, you'll be fine.
(tearfully singing nursery song)
"Wawa, wawa, no more fear,
Mama coming, mama is here
Hush Hush, no more tears
In our hearts forever near . . . "

ART

(to EMTs)
It's her hip.
I think it's broken.

LuLING

(to Ruth only)
My heart,
broken, too.

EMTs start to take LuLing away on a stretcher and Ruth is still holding on to LuLing's hand. But now their hands are pulled apart, and they still reach toward one another, and then LuLing is gone, and the loss of this moment wrenches Ruth's heart.

Ruth leans on Art's shoulder and cries.

ART

She'll be fine.

RUTH

I should have seen the signs.

ART

(surprisingly tender, lifts her face)
Darling, listen . . .
You're not guilty.
Your mom's said it a hundred times:
"Kill myself, rather die."
All these years,
You've given in to
her constant need
for proof of love,
her constant threats
like a knife
at your throat,
when proof of love
wasn't enough,
what no child should endure.
She's suffered, true,
But you've suffered, too.
Care for her,
But care for you.

RUTH

Care for me.

ART

(tenderly) Care for you.
(spoken) Not to mention she's losing her mind.

Dim cold fluorescent light up. LuLing is lying still, deathlike, in a hospital bed.

RUTH

I'll take care of her.

ART

(nods)
The best nursing home,
Medicare approved.

Ruth is shocked.

RUTH

(now fiercely, as if standing up for herself for the first time)
My care,
with us.

Light on LuLing in her hospital bed grows brighter, warmer. Art's attitude toward Ruth is no longer consoling as he tries to reason with her. LuLing stirs, sits up slowly to watch.

ART

She'd drive you crazy.
Not to mention me.

LuLing stiffens, balls fist. Ruth does same.

RUTH

(passionately)
If she dies, I'll kill myself!
I'd rather die.

ART

(shocked)
Ruth, is that a threat?
You're scaring me, Ruth.
You're sounding just like her.

This remark stuns Ruth. LuLing looks puzzled.

RUTH

>I swore I'd never be like her.
>*(wild-eyed)* She's in me.
>Her shards are in my brain.
>Hot glue in my heart.
>Blood from her wounds
>clogging my veins,
>choking my throat.
>*(coming unhinged)* I can't scream loud enough
>To get her out.
>I won't ever kill myself.
>She'll kill me first.

Suddenly exhausted, Ruth slumps into the chair where her mother sat and picks up the mink coat from the floor where LuLing threw it. She looks at it vacantly. Ruth shakes her head, mirroring LuLing as she shakes her head.

ART

>You're tired.
>That's all.
>Take a rest.
>I'll get the car.

Art exits.

Spotlight on Ruth, now alone. She hugs the mink coat and uses a sleeve to caress one side of her face.

RUTH

>*(rocking back and forth in her chair, clutching the mink)*
>I won't ever kill myself . . .
>I won't . . . ever . . .
>don't . . .
>Don't.

Ruth does not see the shadowy figure is approaching in silence.

TRANSITION: BETWEEN WORLDS

As the shadow bends down and brushes her fingers across Ruth's cheek, suona sounds. *Ruth, nervous, quickly glances around.*

RUTH
Ma?

She now opens her eyes and turns toward the shadowy figure.

Who are you?

A warm light illuminates the figure and now we see it is Precious Auntie, whose mouth now appears whole and healed, kneels behind Ruth. Her clothes are a golden yellow in the light. In the background, a Taoist Priest enters.

TAOIST PRIEST
Xian you
Zhi qian
Hui jia
Yi zhuan
(Translation roughly: Before the dead ascend to heaven, they must return home)

While the Priest chants, Precious Auntie takes the mink coat off Ruth's shoulders, and begins to dress her in traditional Chinese clothing, including a red Chinese long jacket, similar in color to what LuLing was wearing at the dinner. She sweeps Ruth's hair into a bun, transforming her into Young LuLing.

RUTH
(turns around)
Who are they?

PRECIOUS AUNTIE
(speak-sing as in Chinese opera)
A body must always return home.

RUTH
Where is home?

PRECIOUS AUNTIE
Immortal Heart.

A procession of The Dead appears wrapped in white cloth resembling wriggling cocoons. The dead leap acrobatically in the air, in rhythm to funeral music, as they follow the Taoist Priest toward Immortal Heart.

Ruth / Young LuLing and Precious Auntie walk behind the leaping dead.

TAOIST PRIEST AND THE DEAD
(call and response in Chinese)
Xian you
Zhi qian
Hui jia
Yi zhuan
(Translation roughly: Before the dead ascend to heaven, they must return home)

As the procession approaches the village, people nearby flee and hide, covering their eyes. Ruth / Young LuLing and Precious Auntie are caught in the melee and carried off-stage.

The Taoist Priest and The Dead arrive at the outskirts of the Village of Immortal Heart, where a large man, Chang the Coffin Maker, filled with self-importance, stands at the head of a gigantic coffin. Wailing Men and Women Mourners in coarse white garments are there to meet The Dead.

CHORUS OF WOMEN MOURNERS
(overlaps Chinese chanting of dead)
The dead must return home
Before the dead ascend to heaven.
The dead. The dead.
Remember the dead.

Chang directs the bodies like a maitre d' to jump into the coffin as the chorus sings. When the last have jumped in, he directs two workers to place the lid on. Now mourners rush forward, bearing funerary objects, and prostrate themselves in poses of hyperbolic mourning and wailing. They place calligraphed white paper banners and bowls of peaches on top.

CHORUS OF MEN MOURNERS
(adding to cacophony)
The dead have returned home
To Immortal Heart
Where blood first flowed
Where blood last flowed
The dead are remembered,
The living dare not forget.

CHANG
(full of self-importance)
The dead must return home
And ascend to heaven
Buried in the coffins by Chang.

Chang pats the coffin proudly.

SCENE 2
IMMORTAL HEART

A SMALL VILLAGE ON THE OUTSKIRTS OF BEIJING⸗
CIRCA LATE 1930S

PART ONE ⸗ CHANG

Mourners turn over sums of money to Chang. Chang points to the coffin and to a pile of lumber that are his materials, displayed by his lackey as he talks of its virtues.

CHANG
In coffins by Chang,
the dead go to heaven
without shame, without fear
they'll be cast into the worst place,
where the poor,
the fools,
and the foreigners live.

*Chang demands more and more, tapping fingers of the right hand in his left—
a gambling gesture—and Mourners painfully hand over more money.*

CHANG
In coffins by Chang
The dead ascend to heaven.

*The head of one of the Dead pushes up the coffin lid; Lackey quickly shoves it
back down.*

More silver, the wood is better.
More gold, the wood is best.

*Another head pops up, is quickly pushed down. Then another pops up. Lackey sits
on the coffin to keep the Dead down.*

No cracks, no bugs, no rot,
Eh? You want a ghost
to stink your house,
Grab your sons,
Steal your wife?
"Why so cheap?" the ghost will wail.
"Why so cheap?"

*Chang gestures for more money and the Mourners reluctantly hand over more
strings of cash, then pull out their pockets to show they're empty.*

In coffins by Chang.

Chang eyes the money and shakes his head.

A happy ghost will cost you more.

*The Lackey pushes them and holds out his hand, demanding the rest. As the
Mourners busily search for where their last bit of cash is hidden—in the damp
folds of a headrag, in the crotch of a pair of pants, in a soiled shoe, under a
sweaty armpit—Chang walks out of their sight over to a scrap pile. He pisses
with great satisfaction on the wood. He picks up a newly anointed plank and
turns to the Mourners.*

See this color? Gold.
More gold, more fragrant.
Fragrant gold.
Smell this fragrance, old.

The Mourners smell a plank, grimace then smile, satisfied with the stench. They
hand over the last of their dirty money and leave. The smell of their money
causes the Lackey to gag.

CHANG
Everybody needs Chang's old wood.

Chang sweeps off the bowls of food and grabs off the paper banners, which he holds
in his fist, and then in gesture of disrespect, he crumples them and throws them
away. He then orders the Lackey to dissemble the coffin lid barely held together
with glue. As the heads of the Dead slowly rise, the Lackey pushes them down.

The Lackey puts a scarf over his nose, and loads the broken coffin lid into the
cart already piled with scraps. Chang walks toward the ink studio, the Lackey
behind him, pushing the cart.

To the ink studio!
Where Chang's wood will burn to soot
for blackest ink,
for smoothest stroke,
for words that never fade.

PART TWO ⚹ THE INK STUDIO

In the Ink Studio, Chang is greeted by obsequious Household Women.

HOUSEHOLD WOMEN
(to Chang)
Welcome, welcome,
Master Chang.
Have you eaten?

All the women are gracious except for one who wears a scowl. She is Precious
Auntie, the Bonesetter's daughter.

CHANG

Chang has eaten!

He walks past them toward Precious Auntie and says to himself:

I once ate her,
sweet flesh, sour heart.

Precious Auntie spits. Chang laughs.

CHANG

Bitter too!

He derides her:

Who are you to spit?
A vessel for men,
best viewed from behind,
or with your head below.

An authoritative woman, Wang Tai-tai, enters and motions Precious Auntie to unload the golden wood, then leaves. Precious Auntie grimaces at the stench of the peed-on wood. She proceeds to stack wood.

CHANG

No longer good daughter
of a famous man,
The Bonesetter of Immortal Heart.
The Bonesetter's potions of Dragon Bones
mended bones.
He mended mine.

PRECIOUS AUNTIE

(throwing wood onto pile violently)
He should have crushed every stinking, evil bone in your body.
(spoken) You killed him!

Wang Tai-tai throws a rag to Precious Auntie and motions for her to clean the urine stains off the floor, then exits. Precious Auntie spits and wipes the floor. Chang watches with pleasure.

CHANG

> *(to himself)*
> But what of the Dragon Bone,
> the secret stuff
> for longest-lasting life!
> If I eat it, I'll never die.
> *(Sly look, plotting)*
> The slut and the slave-girl know where they're buried.

Chang lecherously eyes the orphan slave-girl, 16-year-old Young LuLing, who looks up and smiles at him.

> Slave-girl, have you eaten?

Chang pulls an apple from his pocket and places it in her hands. Precious Auntie rushes over and grabs Young LuLing and pulls her away.

PRECIOUS AUNTIE

> LuLing!

She tries to wrestle the apple from Young LuLing's hands.

YOUNG LULING

> Precious Auntie, I'm hungry!

PRECIOUS AUNTIE

> I'd rather you die than eat his poison.

Jerking the apple out of LuLing's hands, she throws it away.

WANG TAI-TAI

> Faceless One!

PRECIOUS AUNTIE

> *(retreating)*
> Wang Tai-tai.

Wang Tai-tai imperiously gestures for Precious Auntie to resume work, then indicates to all to begin the ink-making.

Chang sneaks LuLing another apple, and winks at her. She grins back broadly and slips it into her pocket.

CHORUS
> Light the fire!
> Make it spit.

Chang gestures with a nod toward LuLing and whispers in Wang Tai-tai's ear. Wang Tai-tai looks at LuLing, who is polishing her apple. She looks at him as if to ask, "You mean her?" He nods.

CHORUS
> Thicken lampblack
> With deerhorn glue.
> Bring out molds
> shaped like moons.
> When no one's looking,
> add a pinch *(pats the stinky wood)*
> Of genuine
> ancient
> secret stuff.

Wang Tai-tai is doing fast calculations on an abacus, shows it to Chang. Chang adjusts the abacus, and shows it to Wang Tai-tai, who acts as if she must relent. Chang writes down agreement.

CHANG
> Wang Tai-tai.

Wang Tai-tai signs it and does an ink dab with her thumb to seal the deal.

WANG TAI-TAI
> Master Chang.

CHORUS
> Thicken lampblack
> With deerhorn glue.
> Bring out molds
> shaped like moons.

Wang Tai-tai hands over the contract to Chang.

WANG TAI-TAI and CHANG
>Longest-Lasting
>Blackest Ink.

CHANG
>*(blowing on paper to dry ink)*
>Words that never fade.

CHORUS
>When no one's looking,
>add a pinch *(pats the stinky wood)*
>Of genuine
>ancient

>*Wang Tai-tai looks appreciatively at Chang, having struck some sort of secret deal.*

WANG TAI-TAI
>Genuine ancient *cheaper* stuff!

CHORUS
>A thousand years old
>So we're told.

CHANG
>*(looking lustily at LuLing)*
>Rrrrrrr.
>A bargain!

CHORUS
>Genuine
>ancient
>secret stuff.

>*Precious Auntie, sensing a deal has been struck that might involve LuLing, stops working.*

WANG TAI-TAI
>*(to LuLing)*
>Slave-girl, stay.

Chang and Wang Tai-tai, in earnest conversation, walk out. The other women also leave, and an angry Precious Auntie begins to draw labels while a petulant LuLing sits idly.

Young LuLing knocks over a box. She bends over to pick it up, and the forbidden apple rolls out of her pocket. Precious Auntie angrily yanks the apple away from her.

YOUNG LuLING
    I hate you!

Precious Auntie slaps Young LuLing, hard.

    Everybody hates you!

PRECIOUS AUNTIE
    Look at these hands.
    Once tender.
    Once soft.

    When you were a baby,
    a pot of boiling soup
    nearly fell upon your head.
    I made my hands into a bowl.
    The blisters lasted
    nearly a year.
    Didn't matter.

    When you were feverish
    One winter night,
    I warmed an icicle
    between my palms,
    drop by drop,
    into your wailing mouth.
    My hands turned blue,
    My fingernails nearly fell off.
    Didn't matter.

    When you were five,
    I showed you bones

From the Dragon Cave,
My family secret
for a thousand years.

We lowered ourselves
through brambles,
and gullies,
past snakes
and thorns
into the Bottom of the World.
I lay on my stomach,
you rode my back,
as I slithered like a worm
into the lightless tunnel,
I clawed out a bone,
So rare!
And offered it to you.
You didn't care.
I told myself,
Be patient. Wait.
One day she will know,
One day she'll know
What is rare,
what is genuine,
what is longest-lasting
secret stuff.

(hopefully to LuLing)
I made my hands into a bowl . . .

*Young LuLing looks up at Precious Auntie. It appears she has understood all
that Precious Auntie has told her. At this moment, Wang Tai-tai rushes back.
She holds a glamorous red wedding dress.*

WANG TAI-TAI
    LuLing, come!

*Young LuLing, wide-eyed, breaks loose of Precious Auntie's grasp and grabs the
garment, hugging it to her chest, and runs off. Wang Tai-tai glances at Precious
Auntie, then exits. Precious Auntie collapses.*

PART THREE ⸺ THE WEDDING

Boisterous shouts and firecrackers erupt. A crowd arrives, a feast is already underway. Raucous, wild music plays, and then comes the wedding anthem and order falls into place as everyone sings together and toasts.

CHORUS

Happy, happy,
Happy, happy,
Today
Two join
To become
One happy happy family.
A sweet young bride.
A handsome groom.
And soon
Son after son after son after many many sons!
We drink to the Happy Family!

Catties of wine,
All that you wish,
heavensent crab,
a fine roasted pig,
and seventeen ducks, what luck.
A feast for all,
all that you wish.
Drink to the Happy Family!

Chang strides by with his Three Wives and Children.

All that you wish
is Chang's.
Three sons, count them.
Chang's.
Three wives,
young,
at one time,
All that you wish is Chang's.
Beauties,

at one time.
Chang's.
And now a bride.
A sweet young bride,
So young.

A wedding sedan led by two suonas *and followed by clanging cymbals and drums arrives. A girl with a red veil is helped out, and her veil sways revealing her face.*

Young LuLing is ushered by women (Chorus and Wives) into a chamber across from the ink studio. They take off her red veil. She is giddy, glowing with wonder and happiness that all this fuss is about her. They add rouge and lipstick to her face. She wears a big smile and acts like an excited little girl. The women take a long gleaming silver hairpin and wind up her hair. The women step back to reveal the transformation. Young LuLing is a sophisticated young woman, grace-ful in her movements and elegant, until she sees herself in the mirror and giggles and acts girlish.

HOUSEHOLD WOMEN
 Her luck has changed!
 Her luck has changed.

CHANG'S THREE WIVES
 Poor girl.
 Her luck has changed.

YOUNG LuLING
 My luck has changed.
 My luck has changed.
 Today not a slave,
 Today a bride!

CHANG'S THREE WIVES
 Poor girl.

YOUNG LuLING
 My luck has changed.

Precious Auntie runs into the wedding chamber. Other women quickly leave.

YOUNG LuLING
(unhearing, deliriously happy)
My luck has changed!

PRECIOUS AUNTIE
For worse.

YOUNG LuLING
My luck has changed!

PRECIOUS AUNTIE
Far worse.

YOUNG LuLING
Costly gold!
My luck has changed.

PRECIOUS AUNTIE
Worse, worse.
Chang's slave-bride!
Worse!
It'll cost you your life.
There are things . . .

Old LuLing appears, illuminated in the distance in her hospital gown.

OLD LuLING
(overlapping Precious Auntie)
These are the things . . .

PRECIOUS AUNTIE
I know are true.

YOUNG LuLING
What you know,
I already know.
Wang Tai-tai told me,
How you once dreamed
dreamed, dreamed
To be the bride
Of Chang.

PRECIOUS AUNTIE
    Never!

YOUNG LuLING
    Wang Tai-tai told me,

PRECIOUS AUNTIE
    Never!

YOUNG LuLING
    How you once led him
    to your bed.

PRECIOUS AUNTIE
    (flapping hands, agitated)
    Never!

YOUNG LuLING
    Wang Tai-tai told me.

PRECIOUS AUNTIE
    NO!
    Wang Tai-tai never told you
    How Chang killed my father,
    How Chang grabbed my neck,
    Chang threw down my honor
    like spit on pig shit!
    For what Chang wanted,
    What your Precious Auntie hid.
    What is rare.
    What is genuine.
    What is longest-lasting life.

Precious Auntie takes from her pocket something wrapped in beautiful cloth, and unfolds it and reveals the Dragon Bone. She does a cherishing gesture to show how valuable it is. Young LuLing stares at it with wonder.

    (now tenderly)
    See these cracks,

See these words?
Written with lightning
by the gods,
given by my ancestors
to my father.

YOUNG LuLING
I see
these cracks, these words.
Written with lightning
by the gods.

PRECIOUS AUNTIE
Given by my ancestors
to my father.

YOUNG LuLING
Your ancestors, your father.

PRECIOUS AUNTIE
and he to me,
now me to you,

YOUNG LuLING
now you to me.

PRECIOUS AUNTIE
What is in your bones.

YOUNG LuLING
A Dragon Bone.
What my husband wanted most
For my dowry.

Precious Auntie suddenly rushes toward Young LuLing and aims the Dragon Bone at her throat. From the shadows, Old LuLing appears in the chamber in her hospital gown, watching this memory, trying to make sense of it. She stands next to Young LuLing, her doppelganger, and mirrors her movements. Young LuLing does not back down, then makes herself look completely empty of fear, a smile on her face.

THE BONESETTER'S DAUGHTER 173

YOUNG LuLING
> Go ahead.
> Do it.
> Right now.

Precious Auntie has the look of a madwoman. Old LuLing takes a step back, clutches her hands to her chest, as if to protect her heart.

OLD LuLING
> I want to live.
> I want to live.

YOUNG LuLING
> *(chantlike at first, as if hypnotized by Old LuLing, then pleading, finally hysterical)*
> I want to live.
> I want to live!
> Please! Let me live!

Precious Auntie, hands shaking, runs out of the room. Old LuLing begins to follow her but stays with Young LuLing, who is hunched over, weeping.

YOUNG LuLING
> My Precious Auntie!
> Don't you love me anymore?

OLD LuLING
> *(pounding her heart)*
> My Precious Auntie!
> Loved me more than she could bear.

A crowd of people rush in and people surround Young LuLing to take her to the wedding. Her veil is placed over her head, covering her face. In this swarm, Old LuLing is swallowed up and disappears.

CHORUS
> Happy, happy,
> Happy, happy,
> We drink to the Happy Family!

Taoist Priest signals for Chang and Young LuLing to approach the altar where there are two large paintings of ancestors with mean faces, male and female, that look exactly like Chang.

Taoist Priest orders them to kneel on the two cushions before the altar.

This is a family
That will live forever.

Young LuLing bows, touching forehead to ground while kneeling on a cushion. Precious Auntie enters, brandishing the dragon bone like a weapon.

CROWD
Careful!

Precious Auntie looks at Chang, then strikes the Dragon Bone against the ground. It bursts into flame.

CROWD
Watch out!

YOUNG LULING
(tilts back her veil, then screams)
NOOOOOOOOOO!

PRECIOUS AUNTIE
A toast to your ancestors.
Let them roast
like pigs.

As Chang and the crowd angrily move toward her, Precious Auntie shakes the fiery bone at them. They reel back, murmuring in alarm.

PRECIOUS AUNTIE
(to Chang at first, then to all others, pointing to each)
From you
I've swallowed
too much hate.
Now I vomit it
on your face,
Vomit on your family,

Vomit
the rest of your days,
No rest from vomit!
(to LuLing)
I drink to save your life.

Chang's family reacts with growing horror as the litany continues.

Marry this girl,
and a ghost will dwell
in your house, in your bed.
You'll never sleep
except with snakes,
toads,
scorpions,
and rats.

Sit on your pot,
grunt all you can,
you cannot move your bowels.
Sit in your bath.
Leeches will suck
your cock of all
your slimy fluids.

Then you'll see
what a ghost foretells:
Your daughters will invite
foreigners to their bed.
Your grandsons will have
ghost-blue eyes.
They'll sail to America
and change their name.
No daughters to weep
or sweep your ash.
No sons to burn offerings,
no comfort or peace
in the land of shades.
If you marry this girl,

Only this curse,
I guarantee.
For I will be
that haunting ghost.
Burning your mind.
Burning your house.
Burning your future.
Burning, burning, burning,
your whole world destroyed,
black as ink,
this longest-lasting curse.

Precious Auntie holds the burning Dragon Bone toward her face. Her mouth becomes a bowl of fire. The flames shoot up and Leaping Ghosts dance with them, as Precious Auntie rises and grows larger. Everyone falls to the ground except LuLing who watches in horror as Precious Auntie is consumed by fire. Ashamed, Young LuLing goes to the flames to reclaim the Dragon Bone. Soon the entire village is engulfed in fire. The ground is shaking, lightning cuts the sky, and sounds of destruction are deafening.

The old world is destroyed.

END ACT 1

ACT **11**

PROLOGUE *
A TIMELESS VOID

PAST MERGED WITH PRESENT

Spotlight on Precious Auntie, her face disfigured. In the style of Chinese ghost women, she is dressed in a flowing tattered gown, her disheveled hair hanging to her knees. She is suspended high, trapped in the World of Yin, pushing against a web, and part of her melted flesh sticks to the web. Trying to find a way out, she creates more tangles with her sticky flesh. She lets out an unearthly moan.

PRECIOUS AUNTIE
(in wild pain)
Fire didn't burn me pure.
Fire didn't make me less.
Fire made me more.
My ashes floating everywhere.
Embers of blood.
Glue of my flesh
Melts and thickens.
Still burning hot.

Spotlight on Young LuLing (Ruth). She is dressed in a simple outfit of the 1940s, holding a scuffed-up suitcase. She walks timidly, as if not certain which way to go. Young LuLing takes out an apple from her pocket, but before she can eat it, she accidentally drops it and it rolls away. She is too tired to find it.

YOUNG LULING
I am no one.
I am no one to no one.
I have no where to go to,
No one to go to.
No one.

Spotlight on Old LuLing lying in a hospital bed suspended in the air. She sits up slowly, looks at her surroundings and appears confused. She screams. None of the women see each other.

OLD LuLING

   Am I past living?
   No one to tell me.
   How can the past not be past?
   I must go there *(she points toward blackness)*
   The moment after this one.

   (she pulls on the flesh of her arm)
   Is this ghost flesh?
   (she pinches) Ai!
   Why does it hurt to be dead?

SCENE 1

HONG KONG HARBOR ⚹ 1940S

Crowds of people swell with the tides of unknown fates. They are of all ages, all backgrounds, all classes: army officers, merchants, bankers, students, fortune-tellers, and actresses, as well as servants, teachers, children, and grannies. As the crowd shifts, Young LuLing becomes visible, still holding on to her suitcase, buffeted as people go one way and then the other.

Ship horns bray, calling for departure and punctuating the panic of people who move toward any hint of opportunity: ticket booths with changing departure information, scam artists claiming to have black-market tickets, and fortune-tellers selling good luck. In contrast, a family of British colonialists board as if going on holiday. As departures get crossed off, opportunities evaporate, and individual families make on-the-spot sacrifices and promises, the consequences of which will be felt for many generations to come.

CHORUS OF MEN AND WOMEN

   My fate has changed.
   My fate has changed.
   The gods spit on me and laugh.

And now I'm stuck in Hong Kong.
No other choice.
No other chance.
No luck at mah jong.
And now I'm stuck in Hong Kong.

No bigshot deals.
No favors to collect.
No help from Auntie in America.
It's up to me
to find my opportunity.

YOUNG LuLING

My fate has changed.
My fate has changed.
No help from Precious Auntie.
And now I'm stuck in Hong Kong.
Should I pray for luck?
Which god? Which goddess?
Should I pray to the Yankee God?
What for?

*Amid the crowd, Chang the Coffin Maker lurks. He has spotted Young LuLing
and shadows her from a distance.*

Can I find a husband
to take me to America?

CHORUS

Stuck, stuck in Hong Kong.

YOUNG LuLING

It's up to me
To find my opportunity.

Taoist Priest appears in the crowd.

TAOIST PRIEST

Passage to America!
What's your best offer?

OLD LuLING
(remembering)
Passage to America . . .

PRECIOUS AUNTIE
My ashes floating everywhere.
Embers of blood.
Still burning hot.

OLD LuLING
Am I past living?
No one to tell me.
How can the past not be past?

YOUNG LuLING
I am no one to no one.

CHORUS AND YOUNG LuLING
My fate has changed.
My fate has changed.
The gods spit on me and laugh.
And now I'm stuck.
No bargains for hope.
No bargains for luck.
No Bargains!

TAOIST PRIEST
Passage . . .

YOUNG LuLING
Can I find a husband
to take me to America?

TAOIST PRIEST
Passage to America!

CHORUS
Stuck, stuck in Hong Kong.

Men break from their wives and children, who are tugging at their sleeves or crying to keep them from leaving. The men pull away, some with great sorrow, and some with pretty young wives and sons by their side, as they speak to their first wives and daughters.

RICH DEPARTING HUSBANDS
> Sons first,
> Daughters later.
> Only one wife
> What can I do?

ABANDONED WIVES
> How can you leave us?

RICH DEPARTING HUSBANDS
> The fates have chosen.
> I have no choice.

Men leave. Abandoned wives are devastated, lost. One well-to-do wife holding the hands of two young daughters walks over to stacks of crates by the harbor, and sits down on a box near where LuLing is. LuLing sees her opportunity, opens her valise, and on the inside case is an advertisement for writing services. She pulls out nice paper and ink brush, poised to work.

YOUNG LuLING
> Letters to America
> Letters to husbands
> So they won't forget.

Woman looks hopeful.

> I can write for you,
> speak for you,
> tell him your hopes.
> Five years experience,
> Written with longest-lasting
> Strongest ink,
> Words that never fade.

She fishes out sample letter.

First letter.
Dear Beloved Husband,
How happy, happy, happy the day
We live in a Yankee-garden house
where I cook your favorite fishes,
where I serve your every wish!
Is this too much to hope for?
Your devoted, grateful wife.

Abandoned Wife leans toward LuLing with great hope and expectation. She hangs on to every word.

Second letter, if he is slow to reply.
Dear Busy Husband,
So many months
Since our happy family
Was happy by your side.
How we miss you,
Your letters, too.
We know you're busy
earning big money
To bring us together
At last and forever.
Your gentle-reminding faithful wife.

Abandoned Wife pictures this and hangs on to every word but somewhat worried, confirming with nods when LuLing has expressed the idea exactly.

Third letter, if he takes a new wife.

Abandoned Wife goes shell-shocked, envisioning this likely impending disaster. She mirrors the desperation, then rage, in the letter.

Dear Sail-Away Husband,
Bound by heaven's fate.
I yank the rope
That ties us.
You will never forget
Your daughters' mouths are empty.
Tell us to stop hoping

So we won't wait
To kill ourselves
And come to you
As ghosts in your bed
Beside your young bride.
Your never-forgetting soon-dead wife.

(spoken) Sometimes it works.

Abandoned Wife, crying, fishes out a pitiful amount of change from her purse. LuLing realizes how tragic her situation is. She waves off the woman's money.

YOUNG LULING
My gift to you.

The sky darkens suddenly and erupts with the crash of thunder, crackling lightning, and gusty wind that blows away the letters.

ABANDONED WIFE
(shouts to children clutched beside her)
Let's go home!

People flee, including people off in the distance. Young LuLing, now alone, stares off in the direction of the woman.

YOUNG LULING
Home. Home . . .

Rain pours down. Young LuLing is now alone. She feels the Dragon Bone in her pocket, fishes it out, and caresses it, remembering, as she gets soaked.

The rain stops. Young LuLing hears the scrape of boxes behind her, and quickly puts the Dragon Bone back in her pocket. The voice of an unseen man calls out, sweet and gentle.

CHANG
(cooing)
Write for me.
Speak for me.
Remember my hopes.

Young LuLing seems puzzled, the words seeming familiar, but not yet recogniz-
able. Precious Auntie is in a frenzy, screaming, but not heard. Old LuLing is in
restless sleep, batting at demons.

A love letter, please
To my wife-to-be,
Who still is not,
Who still will be.
Dear Promised Treasure,
Five years have passed
since that almost happy day.
How weak I was to let you go.
Each day, I say,
You belong to me.

Young LuLing starts to recognize what this is about. Precious Auntie shouts in fury.
Old LuLing sits up, stares down, and starts mirroring gestures of Young LuLing.

Your peach-plump cheeks.
Your rose-bloom lips,
your bell-sway walk,
your shy-look eyes.
All of you belongs to me.

Young LuLing now knows for certain it is Chang. Old LuLing is reliving the memory.
Chang steps out to Young LuLing's horror. She turns to back away, but trips on
her valise and falls. Precious Auntie is agitated, (soundless) screaming. She
pushes against her web.

CHANG
Your quick-beat heart,
Your leap-quick feet,
How fast they run
when you see me!
Oh dearest, how sweet.
Your tears,
Your wonder,
The circle of surprise
on your speechless mouth.

He grabs her and lifts her.

I lift you high,
Hold your face in my hands,
Run my fingers through your hair,
Then down your neck.
Behold your breasts!
Once unripe kumquats,
Now passion-juicy fruit.
Your child-thin legs
Now plump-dumpling thighs.
Come, let me fill that hole
in your heart.
All the holes,
one by one.
Every hole
belongs to me.

Chang drags LuLing by her hair toward the crates. He shoves some of them behind and reveals one of his famous coffins.

At last,
our wedding bed!
Beside you
Above you
On top of you
Behind you.

He starts to pull her toward the coffin but she whips around and holds a sharp object in front of his face. It's the Dragon Bone. She threatens to stab him with it. Chang lets go of her, stares at the Dragon Bone. It seems Young LuLing has successfully fended him off. But then he laughs and simply grabs the bone out of her hand. He laughs long and hard.

The Dragon Bone!
Longest Lasting Life!

Chang grabs Young LuLing again and as she struggles mightily, trying to kick and scratch, he puts the Dragon Bone's sharp edge to her neck. He picks her up, and Young LuLing no longer struggles and allows herself to be laid atop the coffin. As he undresses her, Old LuLing slowly begins to recall what happened, speaking the thoughts of Young LuLing as she watches from her floating hospital bed.

OLD LuLING
> That coffin man
> He climb on me,
> Laughing at my fate.
> I told myself
> Hide yourself
> Close your eyes
> Close your mind.
> Waiting.
> Both of me waiting
> To be split in half.

Precious Auntie breaks out of her web, flies toward Chang, and knocks him off Young LuLing and to the ground. Young LuLing sits up and sees Precious Auntie.

OLD LuLING
> My Precious Auntie—

YOUNG LuLING
> *(with awe)*
> My Precious Auntie!

OLD LuLING
> Wah!
> She grab his face.

YOUNG LuLING
> Grab his face

OLD LuLING
> Put bone to flesh

Precious Auntie holds the Dragon Bone to Chang's nose.

YOUNG LuLING
> Bone to flesh

OLD LuLING
> And pull acrossssss

YOUNG LuLING
> Pull acrosssss

PRECIOUS AUNTIE
> Pull acrossssss—ZZZZT! *(slices off nose)*

Chang wails in pain.

OLD LuLING
> And oh so awful *(mirroring his horror)*
> So much blood

YOUNG LuLING
> So much blood

OLD LuLING
> Pouring out

YOUNG LuLING
> Pouring out

OLD LuLING
> Pouring on the ground.

YOUNG LuLING
> Pouring

PRECIOUS AUNTIE
> Confess!
> What evil you did to
> my father!

Chang backs away.

CHANG
I killed him!

Precious Auntie slices one side of his mouth and up to his cheek.

PRECIOUS AUNTIE
Confess!

YOUNG LuLING, OLD LuLING
Confess!

PRECIOUS AUNTIE
What evil you did
To me.

Chang backs farther away.

CHANG
I raped you.

Precious Auntie draws the Dragon Bone against his nipples and slices across. Blood runs down, covering his chest. Chang writhes and doubles over.

PRECIOUS AUNTIE
Confess!

YOUNG LuLING, OLD LuLING
Confess!

PRECIOUS AUNTIE
What evil you are doing
To my daughter!

YOUNG LuLING
Her daughter?

OLD LuLING
My mother.

YOUNG LuLING
My mother.
Mama.

PRECIOUS AUNTIE
>What evil you are doing
>To your daughter.

Young LuLing is horrified and brings her hands to her mouth, as if to vomit. Old LuLing mirrors this reaction.

OLD LULING
>*(spits, with anger and disgust)*
>His daughter.
>And never will be.

YOUNG LULING
>Never will be.

OLD LULING
>My father.
>And never will be.

YOUNG LULING
>Never ever will be.

PRECIOUS AUNTIE
>Never will be.

Chang backs away farther, making begging gestures. Precious Auntie slices across his belly. When Chang cannot back up any farther, Precious Auntie points the Dragon Bone to Chang's crotch.

OLD LULING
>And Coffin Man
>He scream
>so scared.
>No, no!
>Not little brother!

CHANG
>No!
>Not little brother!

OLD LuLING
   My Precious Auntie,

YOUNG LuLING
   My Precious Auntie,

OLD LuLING
   She took that bone

YOUNG LuLING
   Take that bone.

OLD LuLING
   Still dripping blood.

YOUNG LuLING
   Dripping blood.

OLD LuLING
   And pull acrossssss

YOUNG LuLING
   Pull acrossssss

PRECIOUS AUNTIE
   Pull acrossssss—ZZZZT! *(slices his crotch)*

Young LuLing covers her eyes with her hands. The crotch of Chang's pants darkens with blood. Chang falls to the ground, clutching his crotch, then falls onto his back, and a pool of blood surrounds him. Precious Auntie goes to Young LuLing, whose eyes are still covered.

PRECIOUS AUNTIE
   (singing to Young LuLing)
   Wawa, wawa
   No more fear.
   Mama coming.
   Mama is here.

Old LuLing's hospital bed descends toward Young LuLing and Precious Auntie.

OLD LuLING
  Mama is coming.
  Mama is here.

YOUNG LuLING
  Mama.

PRECIOUS AUNTIE
  Hush, hush.

OLD LuLING
  Hush.

PRECIOUS AUNTIE
  No more tears,

PRECIOUS AUNTIE, OLD LuLING, YOUNG LuLING
  In our Immortal Heart
  Forever near.

In a trio of shared understanding, the women speak what they know is true, who they are to each other, who they are together, how they are one. As they sing, the Past slides into the Present, and Young LuLing becomes Ruth again.

PRECIOUS AUNTIE, OLD LuLING, YOUNG LuLING/RUTH
  These are the things.
  These are the things I know.
  Pain and regret and sorrow.
  Desire and hope and love.
  These things I have known,
  But not enough.
  Not long enough.
  If only I could remember them all.
  These are the things.
  These are the things I know.
  These are the things I know are true.

RUTH
  My name is Ruth Luyi Young Kamen.

LuLing
> Lootie!

Ruth
> I was born in Immortal Heart
> At the Mouth of the Mountain,

LuLing
> The Mouth of the Mountain,

Ruth
> A mouth that swallows up bones
> And spits them out.

LuLing
> Swallows up bones . . .

Ruth
> My mother was the daughter of the daughter of the
> Bonesetter of Immortal Heart,
> And I am the daughter of the daughter
> of the Bonesetter's Daughter.

LuLing
> I am the daughter
> of the Bonesetter's Daughter.

Precious Auntie
> I am a ghost now.
> I live in memory.
> A ghost does not live only in the past.
> You see me, don't you?
> Don't you?

Ruth
> I see you.
> I see me.

Precious Auntie, LuLing, Ruth
> I am the past.
> I am the present.

I am the future.
I am like the village where I was born.

RUTH
Immortal Heart.

LULING
Immortal Heart.

PRECIOUS AUNTIE
Immortal

PRECIOUS AUNTIE, LULING, RUTH
Immortal Heart.

*Together, Ruth and Precious Auntie help lay LuLing back down to sleep in her
hospital bed. As Ruth arranges LuLing's pillows and bed covers, Precious Auntie
fades into the black.*

SCENE 2

HOSPITAL ROOM ⚹ SAN FRANCISCO, FEBRUARY 1997

*LuLing begins to rouse. She is disoriented, confused, tossing and turning in her
hospital bed, seemingly surprised to see Ruth.*

LULING
(confused)
Am I still here?
Where is here?

She looks around and grows panicky. Ruth comforts her, holding her hand.

RUTH
I'm here. I'm here.

LULING
Lootie? Where?
I don't know where I am.

My body so light, like inside clouds.
My memory floating.
Floating away.
So many things,
Like Ghosts,
Gone but still here.

She realizes something horrific, becomes scared like a lost child.

Mama!
Where she gone?
Mama, mama!
MAMA!
(like a relieved child) I wanna see her.
Right now!

LuLing struggles, searching, trying to get out of the bed. Ruth tries to comfort her.

LuLing

Why can't I see her?
Maybe my heart too deep.
I can't see bottom.
Where she is,
Bottom of my heart.
I'm going there now,
Fast as I can.
Sinking so deeply.
Sinking where I can feel
Deeply as you do, Mama.
I'm sorry, Mama.

She stops her rambling, is now connected in the world with Ruth before her. She is anguished, now seeing clearly what happened in the past.

Lootie!
I hurt you
when you were a little girl.

RUTH

>No, Mama . . .

LuLING

>Lootie!
>I scared you.

RUTH

>No, No.

LuLING

>I made you sad,
>I know I did,
>Lootie . . .

RUTH

>Mama . . .

LuLING

>I can't remember . . .
>I can't remember what I did.
>
>I'm telling you, Lootie.
>Sorry.
>So sorry I hurt you.
>And I hope now
>You can forget
>what I've already forgotten.

RUTH

>I've already forgotten, Mama.
>
>*She is crying, happy to have found that they have forgiven each other but also sad that she is about to lose her mother.*

RUTH

>But I will always remember.
>Who you are.
>Who I am.
>What is in our bones.

Ruth kisses LuLing's forehead, strokes her hair, then brushes LuLing's cheek with the back of her hand. From the dark, Precious Auntie's face emerges magnified many times, as if it were composed of a million tiny lights, her blackened mouth healed.

With her hand, LuLing suddenly indicates for Ruth to quickly get the mink coat. Ruth starts to lay it over LuLing like a blanket. LuLing immediately gestures to Precious Auntie. Ruth now sees Precious Auntie and looks at her with awe, placing the mink coat over Precious Auntie's flowing ghostly white robes. Precious Auntie places the Dragon Bone in Ruth's hands.

LuLING

What is secret.
What is rare.
What is true.
My body so light.
Floating away.
I feel so much.

Clutching the Dragon Bone, Ruth watches as her mother and grandmother disappear into the fog.

END

OF OPERA

ACKNOWLEDGMENTS

MAKING THIS OPERA TOOK MORE THAN A VILLAGE.
AMY, STEWART, AND KEN WOULD LIKE TO THANK:

THE CREATIVE TEAM AND THE SAN FRANCISCO OPERA:
Karen Ames, Roberta Bialek, Donato Cabrera, Chen Shi-Zheng, Kip Cranna, David Gockley, Mark Grey, John A. and Cynthia Fry Gunn, Leigh Haas, Han Feng, Drew Landmesser, Marcia Lazer, Mary Powell, John Osterweis and Barbara Ravizza, Ian Robertson, Matthew Shilvock, Steven Sloane, Walter Spangler, Roselyne C. Swig, Scott Zielinski

The Bonesetter's Daughter, THE JOURNEY:
Lavelle Alexa, Elizabeth Andrus, Asia Society, Laura Aswad, Sunny Bates, Jeanette Chang, Joan Chen, Tina Chen, William and Gayle Cook, Rachel Cooper, Eleanor Sebastian and Charles Frank, Gil Cohen and Paul Gervais, Barbara Gimbel, Mike Hearn, Heather Hitchens, La Frances Hui, Naomi Kaldor, Michael Korie, Geri Kunstadter, Suzanne Lehmann, Loren Linder, Aenon Loo, Timothy Long, MacDowell Colony, Tim McHenry, Meet the Composer, Emily and David Pottruck, Anupam and Rajika Puri, Elaina Richardson, Pierra Roberts, Rubin Museum, Orville Schell, Marie-Monique and Ray Steckel, Shining Sung, Jack and Joanna Tang, Oscar and Argie Tang, Sarina Tang, Norman and Antonia Tu, Jack and Sandy Turk, Cissy Pao Watari, Clara Weatherall, Fred Wistow, Yaddo, Cheryl Young, Tony and Vivian Zaloom

IN CHINA:
Ai Yingying, Arlene Barilec, Alex Beels, Maureen Chiu, Lee Wai Kit and Isa Chu, Happy Harun, Hong Kong Chinese Orchestra and Yan Huichang, Hu Chaoxiang, Ellen Kaplowitz, Zinnia Kwok, Joanna Lee, Patrick P. Lee, Ciris Leung, Li Yuewu, Liang Chengjian, Liu Feng, Liu Yang, Eli Marshall, Peter Micic, Daniel Ng, Dan Ouyang, Leon Ren, Wu Aixiang, Wu Jingxin, Wu Xiuchun, Xiu Fen, Charlie Yan, Yang Changshu, Yang Shengjuan, Yuen Siu Fai, Zhang Jianshu, Zhang Zhanxian

THE PERFORMERS AND THE MUSICAL TEAM:

Zheng Cao, Cathy Cook, Sally Groves, Shirley Ip, James Kendrick, Lawrence Manchester, Richard Martinez, Li Li, Xiuying Li, Li Zhonghua, Ning Liang, Liu Yang, James Maddalena, Bruce Munson, Niu Jiandang, Qian Yi, Norman Ryan, Hao Jiang Tian, Wu Tong

WITH THE DOCUMENTARY FILM:

Center for Asian American Media, KQED San Francisco, Monica Lam, David Petersen, Fawn Ring

FAMILY AND FRIENDS:

Lou DeMattei, Dianne Festa, Martin Garbus, Angelo Garro, Ted Habte-Gabr, Ann and Gordon Getty, Lisa Iacucci, Martha Liao, Ellen Moore, Geri Palazzi, Michael Tilson Thomas and Joshua Robison, Lucas Kalman Wallace, Sidney and Marsha Wallace, Bill Wu

AT CHRONICLE BOOKS:

Darcy Cohan, Hannah Cox, Susan Coyle, Judith Dunham, Jacob Gardner, Molly Jones, Jennifer Kong, Brad Mead, Nion McEvoy, Doug Ogan, Jay Schaefer, Brianna Smith, Beth Steiner

The Bonesetter's Daughter was commissioned by the San Francisco Opera; David Gockley, general director. The commission and original production were made possible by a generous gift from John A. and Cynthia Fry Gunn. Support for conception and development of the opera was generously provided by *The Bonesetter's Daughter, The Journey*; Sarina Tang, executive producer

World Premiere: September 13, 2008, War Memorial Opera House, San Francisco, California

Music published by SidMar Music (ASCAP), represented worldwide by Schott Music International

Set design by Walter Spangler
Costume design by Han Feng
Chinese brush calligraphy by Patrick P. Lee

譚恩美

惠士劍

STEWART
WALLACE

AMY
TAN